*at*
# Peace
*in the*
# Storm

## Books by Ken Gire

FROM BETHANY HOUSE PUBLISHERS

*Relentless Pursuit*

*At Peace in the Storm*

# *at* PEACE *in the* STORM

*Experiencing the Savior's Presence*
*When You Need Him Most*

KEN GIRE

BETHANY HOUSE PUBLISHERS
*a division of Baker Publishing Group*
Minneapolis, Minnesota

Published by Bethany House Publishers
11400 Hampshire Avenue South
Bloomington, Minnesota 55438
www.bethanyhouse.com

Bethany House Publishers is a division of
Baker Publishing Group, Grand Rapids, Michigan

Printed in the United States of America



Library of Congress Cataloging-in-Publication Data

Gire, Ken.
At peace in the storm : experiencing the Savior's presence when you need him most / Ken Gire.
pages cm
Summary: "An inspirational and thoughtful look at biblical characters and stories that will encourage readers going through difficult times"— Provided by publisher.
ISBN 978-0-7642-0884-3 (pbk. : alk. paper) 1. Peace of mind—Religious aspects—Christianity. 2. Consolation. I. Title.
BV4908.5.G57 2014
248.8′6—dc23 2013026765



Cover design by Greg Jackson, Thinkpen Design, Inc.

Author is represented by WordServe Literary Group

14 15 16 17 18 19 20 7 6 5 4 3 2 1

# Contents

# Introduction

## *Two Kinds of Storm—Calming Miracles*

> If God be our God, He will give us peace in trouble. Where there is a storm without, He will make peace within.
>
> Thomas Watson

We all want the outer, measurable, touch-it, see-it miracle.

We want the child-turned-adult addict to come to the end of himself and head home, his prodigal heart humbled and ready to do whatever it takes to leave the pigsty.

We want spouses with wandering eyes and discontented hearts to break through their mental fog and wake up one morning with the realization: "I've been a fool! I was blind, but now I see. How precious you are! I've hurt and mistreated you, and now I'm going to love and cherish you forever and always."

We want the job to come through, our flaws to disappear, the cancer to go away. And sometimes, thank God, we actually see these miracles. God calms the circumstantial storm and we are relieved and grateful, as our furrowed brows relax and the knots in our gut give way to peace, blessed peace. Joy, unbounded joy. It's finally over. Our prayers are answered. The storm has passed. We've got a testimony wrapped up with a bow, ready to take on the world.

And then there are those pesky chronic storms that linger long, that wear us down, that don't go away. Month after month, year after year, we look on the horizon for the Savior we thought we knew, the One who could walk on water and order the waves stilled and bring instant calm to our lives.

But here's the rub about faith (and most of us who've lived for a while, had a long marriage or lost one, or a few imperfect kids or grandkids, a betrayal or a personal failure, or any number of life's disappointments, know it all too well): Prayer changes things, it calms things *and* us, it soothes and restores. But *what* things are actually changed or restored are not in our hands or under our control.

Though we long for the miracle of the outward variety, the only real guaranteed miracle God offers us is inner peace, the peace of Christ. A peace so deep that it cannot be analyzed or understood. It just descends on us even when everything else is falling apart, while the drug-addicted child does not come to his senses and continues to eat hog slop, the job offer doesn't pan out, the cancer rages, and the marriage is a hollow mess.

But I'll let you in on a secret. This miracle of the inner variety, this inexplicable and supernatural calm in the storm, is the greatest miracle you'll ever experience.

Getting to a place of steady inner calm is not easy. Like any skill, it does get easier to put our auto-panic nature on pause as we learn, and practice, and grow in trust. But life is tough, we are human, and all of us get shaken. Sometimes to the core.

Even Jesus struggled when he was in Gethsemane and peace eluded him. But in that painfully horrific space of time, he eventually experienced calm. And though his circumstances did not change, and the cup he asked to be removed still awaited him, peace descended upon the Savior, and he faced his appointed mission with calm, grace, and courage.

If Jesus struggled in his darkest days to get from despair to calm, then we should not be surprised that the miracle of inner peace is a journey and a process for us too. And it is often two steps forward, one back. So we must be gentle with ourselves, especially when circumstances around us go awry.

I've had my share of storms and despair, some out of the blue, some of my own making. Days when I didn't want to wake up to face another day of disappointing God, others, myself. Even as I write this book, I write to remind myself that there is that peace that passes understanding, even when I am caught in the grip of worry or waves of unworthiness. I've experienced God's peace before, and even if I reel or stumble today, tossed by a dozen white-capped waves, I know his calm will come again. I know Jesus will find me in this frightening, uneasy place, for I remember how he has shown up before—for me and countless others.

He may choose to calm the outer storm or calm the inner me. Either is fine, as long as I get to that place of peace where it is well with my soul. That is the only miracle you or I really need, one day at a time.

The following chapters relate the many creative ways in which God brought peace, calm, and hope to me and many others through frightening, dark, and worrisome hours. I don't know how he will bring the miracle of peace to your heart. I only know that he promises to do it. And that is a good place to begin.

> May the Lord of peace himself give you peace at all times and in every way. The Lord be with all of you.
>
> 2 Thessalonians 3:16

# 1

# Peace Through Perspective

> When a captain trusts a pilot to steer his vessel into port, he manages the vessel according to his direction.[1]
>
> Charles H. Spurgeon

A counselor in the Northeast United States was known to receive many a suffering soul who would come to him for help during a stormy season of life. Each would step into his office with the hope of finding a temporary lifeline of support.

After the initial welcome, he would settle in to a comfortable chair and offer his client a seat on the worn corduroy sofa. He began each session with a new client exactly the same way: He didn't ask what was troubling the person. He didn't unpack any deep childhood trauma. He didn't ask if he or she had been attending church regularly, and although they often reached that point, it wasn't where the session began. Rather, this wise counselor asked the one seeking help just *one question*: When have you encountered the holy presence of God?

He knew that those who are being battered about by life's storms tend to set their eyes on the clouds, scanning the heavens for lightning. We search the water's surface for the next swell. Brace ourselves for the next surge. If we keep our eye on the storm, we figure we'll be able to extricate ourselves from the bind in which we find ourselves. Whether or not we *can* actually deliver ourselves from life's storms, we desperately want to believe that we can.

In asking those in need of help to identify the moment or moments when they experienced God's faithfulness, this wise counselor was inviting them to ground themselves in the faithfulness of God. By naming and finding comfort in the ways God had met them in the past, they were able to sink roots into solid ground. Some spoke of a mountaintop spiritual experience at a summer camp as a teen. Others mentioned quiet moments with the Lord when they had heard God's still, small voice, almost a whisper, in their hearts. Others reported God's palpable presence while breaking bread with other believers. Some reached into the dusty recesses of their memories to recall a spiritual experience of God's living presence they'd long ago dismissed, attributing it to the exuberance of youth or the joy of newfound faith.

When given permission to claim these moments as reliable signs of God's comfort and presence, sufferers found relief. For many, remembering God's provision was a peaceful refuge in the eye of the storm. The life preserver they were offered, and to which they clung, was the memory of God's faithfulness in the past.

## Where Will You Set Your Eyes?

Perhaps the relentless rains in your life have made the earth seem slippery beneath your feet. Adrift, you may feel as if the ground has dropped out from under you. If you're like many, your natural temptation might be to set your eyes on the storm.

If a loved one has received a terrifying diagnosis, you will pore over online research for hours. When finances are tight, you and your spouse review the budget, again and again, trying to make the numbers work. When the world seems to be falling apart, rent asunder by tornado, flood, or terror, you glue your eyes to the television screen, watching the winds work their fury. Impotent, tossed by the waves, you continue to drift.

It's understandable. We want to be able to still the waters. Silence the thunder. Extinguish the lightning. And though the power to quiet the storms that batter and toss you may be out of reach, the lifeline you need, the peace you crave, may be closer than you think.

## An Unlikely Rescue

When ancient Israel was under threat of attack by the great Philistines, they had no illusions that their human power could save them. Two decades earlier, on the battlefield where they now stood in terror, the Philistines had slaughtered thirty thousand Hebrew men (1 Samuel 4:10). Now, trembling, they were vulnerable again.

Though they lacked military might, Samuel was spiritually preparing the people for battle. For years Israel had been unfaithful to God, dabbling in the worship of foreign gods. When the ark of the covenant was returned to Israel, though, they turned their hearts back to the Lord, rejecting the gods they'd worshiped and putting away their idols. Under the leadership of Samuel—in the middle of the battlefield where they'd known such gruesome defeat—they fasted, confessed, and worshiped.

As the mighty Philistines approached Aphek, the site of Israel's earlier tragic defeat, Samuel was offering a burnt sacrifice unto God. As the enemy crept closer toward a repentant people whose hearts were turned toward God, they heard the shouts of the Israelites who were seeing the arrival of the Lord's ark of the covenant, and the thundering roar threw the Philistines into a panic. In the chaos that ensued, the men of Israel were able to pursue and defeat their enemy. In the very spot where they'd once been defeated and robbed of the ark of God, their powerful nemesis was destroyed.

Samuel, an anointed leader and a man of God, knew instinctively that *this* miraculous wonder was a moment to mark in the memory of the Hebrew people. To remember the Lord's gracious intervention, to commemorate the present help of God in their time of need, Samuel erected a stone memorial. He called it *Ebenezer*, meaning "stone of help," saying, "Thus far the LORD has helped us" (1 Samuel 7:12). The stone memorial would serve as a tangible reminder that in the most dire circumstances God intervenes. God saves. God rescues. When the Hebrew people looked on the Ebenezer, located between the cities of Mizpah and Shen, they would be reminded of what God had done for them. The solid rock would come to symbolize God's steadfast reliability on the very darkest days.

## My Ebenezers

Like the Hebrew people, I am able to look back at my journey and recognize a number of shipwrecks in the storms of my life. I have not, however, drowned. I'm still here. With the grace of God and the kindness of friends, I have made it through those storms.

In my childhood home, I saw a visual representation of the steadfast, faithful presence of Jesus. Hanging in our dining room was a print of an oil painting featuring a sailor straining with all his might to steer his vessel through a storm. Beside him, transparent but visible, Jesus was depicted, pointing the way with one hand and resting the other on the sailor's shoulder. Even as a boy, I found comfort in that compelling image. In fact, for me, that painting became a small Ebenezer, a monument to God's faithfulness to another, which would, over time, become etched in my heart as a foretaste of God's own promise to me.

## Commemorating the Faithfulness of Another

Throughout the centuries, human beings have erected grand memorials recognizing remarkable human achievement and pivotal moments in our history. With these impressive structures we celebrate human ingenuity and power: the Egyptian pyramids, France's Palace of Versailles, the Great Wall of China, the Roman Coliseum. We mark the places where powerful human civilizations have been most *godlike.*

We also create memorials to commemorate just the opposite. We mark those places where the sting of death has prevailed. The hulking granite Pennsylvania State Memorial marks the site where 51,000 lives were lost in the Battle of Gettysburg (Civil War, 1863). Today in Berlin, 2,711 concrete blocks evoke the memory of those lives lost in the Holocaust. In New York City, two wide pools glimmer where the World Trade Center once towered above the city.

While naturally inclined to erect both symbols of our greatest successes and our greatest defeats, we have been less likely to mark those occasions when desperate, powerless, and defeated, we were rescued by the mighty hand of Another. We've failed to point to the One who rescues and redeems when we've reached the end of ourselves. And yet the cross of Jesus Christ—the most deeply significant symbol of our faith—is just this type of marker. Erected in sanctuaries, worn on delicate gold chains, emblazoned on tattooed biceps, the cross points to that moment when human evil seemed to have triumphed but where God miraculously, graciously intervened.

The Ebenezer that Samuel erected reminded the Hebrew people that their God rescued and redeemed in the most unlikely circumstances. When other storms would threaten, they could look to the Ebenezer and find comfort, strength, and peace at the memory of God's tangible provision.

## A Past That Predicts the Future

Pastor Robert Robinson understood the significance of naming and remembering the Ebenezers in our lives. In 1757, at the age of twenty-two, he penned the moving lyrics to "Come, Thou Fount of Every Blessing," a hymn of praise and gratitude. Evoking the image of Samuel's Ebenezer, Robinson trumpets God's goodness on the evidence of God's faithfulness in the past:

> Here I'll raise my Ebenezer,
> Hither by Thy help I'm come;
> And I hope by Thy good pleasure
> Safely to arrive at home.

His poetry evokes images of a lifelong journey with God, pointing to God's help in ages past, establishing a testimony to

God's faithfulness in the present and celebrating his confidence that God will continue to guide and lead.

Recently a friend of mine, frustrated by some of the language in the church's more traditional hymns, confided, "I don't even know what an Ebenezer is!"

Though modern adaptations of Robinson's original text have avoided the word *Ebenezer,* finding other words to suggest God's enduring faithfulness, I think the scriptural word is worth hanging onto. When we name and remember the particular moments of God's past deliverances in our lives, we stand once again on the solid ground of God's faithfulness. This is as important as when, pummeled by the storm, we are searching for hope and security.

The next time my friend is tossed on perilous seas, I want her to find the kind of strength I've found by remembering the moments of God's faithfulness to me.

## God's Faithfulness to Me

A few years ago, my grandson, six years old at the time, was living in Colorado for the summer, and I spent a lot of time with him. In fact, I taught him to swim. We enjoyed an outdoor pool as well as an indoor pool at the YMCA.

When he finally got the hang of swimming, he couldn't wait to spend that time with me! I think he could have done it every single day, all day long. We became really good friends during that time. He went from calling me Grandpa to Gramps to Pop. I taught him to float on his back, to do the breaststroke, and the crawl. Eventually he could swim the entire length of the pool by himself. Of course, we played lots of games too, from tag to shark to splashing water at each other, to racing each other, throwing money into the pool and having him find it.

We even went fishing. And though we came up empty-handed, we didn't come up empty-hearted. We caught grasshoppers in Mason jars, and we hiked to the top of my beloved Palmer Lake Reservoir. My grandson was an absolute trooper. Never once did he complain about how long it was or how hard.

I remember one day when we raced inside from a very cold rain and jumped into bed with a pan full of brownies and watched a cooking show on TV (his dad was a cook, so he liked that). That summer we also saw about ten movies together at the local theater. They were all kids' movies, of course, and several of them were in 3-D. We shared snacks, and even played air hockey and video games in the lobby of the theater.

My grandson's presence in my life was a gift.

This was *the* Ebenezer experience for me. It was a season of re-creation that God provided to which I often return in my heart and mind: an entire summer of encounters with God through the boundless energy, unbridled joy, and exuberant adoration of a child. Saturating me with God's peace that passes all understanding, it was a summer that revived and refreshed me in every way and one I will never forget.

## Paul's Assurance of God's Reliability

Every letter Paul wrote in the New Testament begins with a greeting to his readers, wishing them peace. Paul could write confidently about that peace because he had experienced it time and time again. Nowhere did he experience it more than at sea.

Paul states that he was shipwrecked three times, and one of those times he spent a night and a day adrift in the open sea (2 Corinthians 11:25). His voyage to Rome was the most harrowing. He sailed aboard a ship that traveled from harbor to harbor, hugging coastlines along the way, taking soundings to stay out of the shallows, and keeping watch to steer clear of reefs. From weighing anchor to weathering the storms, to wintering at some foreign port, the journey was long and arduous, filled with dangers and uncertainties: adrift with slackened sails, swells lifting them and dropping them. Seasickness. Fear of the unknown day in and day out.

When would the storm end? When would the sea be calm again? Their clothes dry again? Their bodies warm again? When would they get their sea legs back, their strength back, their hope back?

You might know what it's like. *Terror* is too tepid a word to describe it. Panic sets in, and that either sends you into a frenzy of activity or it paralyzes you. You row with all your back, bail with all your heart—or you go belowdecks, curl into a fetal position, close your eyes, and shiver alone in the dark.

Paul was no stranger to turmoil. And when he looked back over his life, when he searched for the Ebenezers that marked God's deliverance, he could point to journey after journey when God rescued, saved, and delivered. When new winds began to blow, he could recall God's faithfulness in storms past. When imprisoned, he could return to God's steadfast provision during previous imprisonments. When persecuted, he could look back and see how God had provided—uniquely in each situation—with the confidence that God could and would come through for him again.

## Marking a Life's Journey

Where are those moments in your journey to which you can point and say, "*That* is where I experienced God's peace"? Were you buoyed with God's *shalom* when the world seemed to be crumbling around you? In the wake of the loss of a loved one, did you have a palpable sense of God's comfort? When you suffered emotionally, did God's faithfulness sustain you? When you suffered financial difficulty, did God meet your needs?

Pause to retrace your journey with God. If you've never taken a thorough inventory of God's faithfulness in your life, this is your chance to erect spiritual stones and to proclaim with boldness, "Thus far the Lord has helped me, and the Lord will help me now." As you do, you may be reminded of the particular verse of Scripture with which the Lord comforted you. You may remember the face of the person God used to care for you and offer a word of peace. You may recognize other resources God provided during your time of need—a doctor, a pastor, a counselor, a friend. Use a journal to record the verses and faces and songs and signs that God has used to grant you his peace that passes all understanding. When you return to those Ebenezers that mark God's faithfulness in your life, you are given fresh eyes to see how God might work again.

Corazon Aquino, elected president of the Philippines after a contested election and revolt in 1986, was the first female president in Asia. She says, "Faith is not simply a patience that passively suffers until the storm is past. Rather, it is a spirit that bears things—with resignations, yes, but above all, with blazing, serene hope." For followers of Christ, the hope with which we bear things, the hope we have in the storm, is one based on the memory of God's faithful provision and deliverance. It is a hope upon which we can rely.

> For great is your love, higher than the heavens; your faithfulness reaches to the skies.
>
> Psalm 108:4

# 2

# Peace Through Prayer

He that will learn to pray, let him go to sea.

George Herbert (1593–1633)

When she was diagnosed with tuberculosis in 1943, Catherine Marshall was married to the pastor of a vibrant Washington, DC congregation and was the mother of a busy toddler. Month after month of chest X-rays suggested the prayers of this woman of great faith were in vain, driving her to despair.

Marshall had read the story of a missionary who had begged God for healing while she was disabled for eight years. It was only when the woman gave up praying for health, and relented to the will of God, that she was healed.

At the end of her own rope, Catherine Marshall emptied herself before the Lord. She explains, "I handed over to God every last vestige of self-will, even my intense desire for complete health. Finally I was able to pray, 'Lord, I understand no part of this, but if You want me to be an invalid for the rest of my life—well, it's up to You. I place myself in Your hands, for better or for worse. I ask only to serve You."[1]

Later that night, Jesus appeared to Marshall, healing her body entirely of tuberculosis.

In the laboratory of human suffering, Marshall discovered a type of prayer that she called the Prayer of Relinquishment. It is the prayer we pray when, exhausted from praying, we release every hope that our circumstance might be different and trust entirely in God's will for us. It is that prayer that says, and truly *means*, "Not my will, but Yours, be done."

It was at sea, battered by life's tsunami, that Catherine Marshall learned to pray.

Countless others who have been touched by her life and witness have prayed this prayer in the darkness of their own stormy nights. One prayed the prayer on a cold, hard table in a radiology room as she awaited test results. Another, who'd been stuck in a desperate professional situation, knelt down in her bedroom and prayed the prayer beside a rocking chair. One prayed it at the bedside of a loved one. Though powerful, it's not a prayer meant to manipulate God. Rather, it is a complete submission to God's will, whatever it may be.

The storm becomes our school of prayer.

## We Learn to Pray at Sea

Bouncing across raging seas, bent to our knees and clinging for safety, is where we learn to pray. Ask Noah, adrift on the swells of the diluvian sea. Ask Jonah, tossed about on the Mediterranean. Ask the disciples, taking on water on the Sea of Galilee. Ask Paul, weathering perilous storms on voyage after voyage.

The storm you're facing may be financial, when you find yourself caught up in a category 4 hurricane that sweeps over the economy like Katrina over the Gulf Coast. Widespread flooding. Levees breaking. Your home underwater. Your family drowning in debt. Standing in water to your waist is where you will learn to pray.

Your storm may be vocational, when your job is outsourced overseas or made obsolete by technology. Wet with tears, your prayers take on new urgency.

The storm you face may be relational, when a friendship turns against you. When a teenager is caught in the vortex of raging hormones, tempestuous emotions, and pressures from peers. When a marriage is broadsided by a rogue wave of infidelity or grounded on a shallow reef that slowly sinks it. Stuck in the mire, you pray.

Your storm may be physical, when your loss of balance turns out to be MS, or the lump turns out to be malignant. It can be emotional, when the undulations of mood plunge you into the depths of depression. Gasping for air, you pray.

The storm in your life may be a spiritual one, when you have been driven and tossed by the wind for so long and you have taken on so much water that you are filled with doubt. You are holding on, but just barely, as wave after wave washes over you. You're gasping for air, heaving your insides out. Your eyes are stinging from all the water, and you can hardly see anything clearly. How much more can you take? How much longer can you hold on?

When your grip is slipping and you are suffocating, you feel as though the very *last* thing you can do is pray.

## Storm Prayers

During these times, I most often pipe short, clipped, desperate prayers: "Save me, Lord!" "Help me." "Please, help me." "Please." In a storm there are no requisite word counts. There is no formal grammar. There are no lofty phrases. The Jesus prayer has just seven words: "Lord Jesus Christ, have mercy on me." Anne Lamott, who seems to pray like me, once identified the two most popular prayers in the world, ostensibly mid-storm and post-storm, as "Help, help, help" and "Thank you, thank you, thank you." The witness of Jesus' own disciples demonstrates that elaborate construction is not necessary:

"Master, don't you care that we are perishing?"

That was the prayer the disciples prayed when the storm swept over their boat and Jesus was asleep in the stern.

"Lord, save me!"

This was the prayer Peter prayed when he stepped out of the boat, taking his eyes off of Jesus and onto the wind and the waves that slapped against him.

The one prayer was a question, the other an exclamation.

In every life there are times when Jesus *does* seem to be asleep in the stern, while our lives are taking on water, and we are breaking our backs, bailing our hearts out. How can he possibly be sleeping? On a cushion, no less! How could he not hear the waves smashing against the hull, not feel the water sloshing over the sides? How could he not see that we are perishing? How could he not care?

We wake him with our prayers, or so it seems. And he is inconvenienced, or so it seems. Even irritated. The question turns the way it did with the widow's question to the unrighteous judge (Luke 18:1–8). And we learn that while we are looking for rescue, he is looking for faith.

It is difficult to be hard on the disciples. What *should* they have done? How *should* they have approached him? Or when?

They didn't come to Jesus until they'd come to the end of themselves. Maybe that is what prompted the rebuke. Maybe they looked at him as their last resort instead of their first. Maybe they didn't want to disturb him, and that is what he wanted them to do most. To come to him first. To realize he would *want* them to come to him first.

Jesus, no doubt, would have gladly received just a single word: "Lord!" "Master!"

There have been a lot of times when I have cried myself to sleep while praying. Not sobbing, just gentle tears spilling from my eyes. When the storm has raged for too long, we are weary. We are out of thoughts. We are out of feelings. We are out of prayers. What then?

When we've reached the end, Jesus simply *receives* us. No words. A sigh. A heaving of your heart toward heaven, however heavy it may be to lift, however hard it may be to heft. When it is too hard, the Holy Spirit will do the heaving, lifting, groaning, to carry it for you.

## My Prayers in the Storm

I remember in high school being at the hospital late at night after my dad's heart surgery. I was the only family member there. I heard a call over the speaker system for members of the Gire family. I was really scared. The cardiologist told me that one of the bypasses had come loose and he was going to have to go back in and try to fix it.

"Is it serious?" I remember asking.

He nodded. I went to the little chapel at Harris Hospital and prayed, cried, and felt peace. Prayer had somehow brought me into the presence of the One who brings peace.

One of the stories of Jesus in prayer, which has brought great comfort to me, is an unlikely one. When I am in need of peace, I join Jesus on his knees in the garden of Gethsemane. In the midst of his own violent storm, about to be seized by Roman authorities, Jesus pauses to pray. Sometimes it takes a lot of sweat, tears, and agony to get to the point of peace, but prayer is what leads us there, just as it led our Lord.

This glimpse of Jesus praying in the storm is reminiscent of Martin Luther's own insistence: "I have so much to do that I shall spend the first three hours in prayer." For Jesus, there wasn't any strategizing to be done with the disciples that was *more* important than prayer, especially as storm clouds gathered.

What makes this scene an unlikely source of comfort is that Jesus *does* drown, in a manner of speaking. It is neither a story of heroic rescue nor of rains that suddenly cease. In the garden, however, Jesus' prayer is still a source of comfort to me. There, he prays a prayer of relinquishment, offering, "Father, if you are willing, take this cup from me; yet not my will, but yours be done" (Luke 22:42). That this was the prayer of Jesus when thunder clapped and winds roared around him, gives me peace to join him in the same prayer.

In his book *Open Hands*, Henri Nouwen describes the way in which our natural tendency is to cling to those things that make us feel safe and secure. Our natural temptation, as waves billow and lightning fills the sky, is to grab onto something for safety. We reach for the side of the boat or a sturdy rope. Our impulse is to anchor ourselves to whatever seems to offer security. The very last thing our clenched fists want to do in a storm is to relax. To release. Yet Nouwen exhorts, "To pray, is to open our hands to God."

Over the years, this is how I've prayed for my children. Sometimes these have been tearful prayers, sometimes desperate prayers, sometimes bargaining prayers. Somehow, with open hands, these prayers have brought me to a place of peace. Not all at once, but eventually. Unclenching our fists, the movement of prayer is to trust with the trust of Jesus. In the same way Jesus fully entrusted himself into the hands of the Father who loved him, so we too are invited to entrust our lives into the hands of the Father who loves us.

## Saint in the Storm

Saint Patrick, the famous saint of Ireland, was actually born in Scotland, in the fourth century. As a teen, he was captured and taken to Ireland as a slave, working as a shepherd. During his captivity, Patrick turned his face and his heart to God, his love and passion for the Lord and for prayer ever increasing. At twenty, in a dream, God instructed Patrick to escape via the sea. Stealing off to the coast, Patrick sailed to safety in Britain.

The comfortable, happy ending to Patrick's story was not to be, as God continued to speak to Patrick through his dreams. In one, the people of Ireland begged him to return to them. After he had studied and was ordained to the priesthood, later ordained as a bishop, Patrick indeed returned to the land of his captivity, full of love for the people he'd come to know during his slavery. As a result of Patrick's forty-year preaching throughout the country, many in the land that was mainly pagan and Druid were converted to the Christian faith.

Patrick had weathered the most brutal of storms through prayer. Just as many have learned how to pray from the prayers Catherine Marshall discovered in her storm, gleaned in desperation from another traveler being battered by wind and waves, so too we may learn the way of prayer from this one who journeyed ahead of us. From one who set his eyes on God in the most cruel circumstances, we receive Saint Patrick's Breastplate Prayer. Receiving its name from Ephesians 6:14, Patrick girded himself in prayer with holy protection by which to weather the storm.

> Christ with me, Christ before me,
> Christ behind me, Christ within me,
> Christ beneath me, Christ above me,
> Christ at my right, Christ at my left,
> Christ in the fort,
> Christ in the chariot seat,
> Christ on the deck,
> Christ in the heart of everyone who thinks of me,
> Christ in the mouth of everyone who speaks to me,
> Christ in every eye that sees me,
> Christ in every ear that hears me.[2]

Patrick prayed with the firm conviction that Christ was *with him*. Christ wasn't watching him suffer from a safe heavenly distance. Christ was with him: shackled, drenched in sea water, shivering, on the deck of the vessel of captivity. Imagine the terror fourteen-year-old Patrick would have felt being kidnapped and taken to a land where he had no kin. Eugene Peterson has written, "We become what we are called to be by praying." In the midst of Patrick's journey, in such a beautiful redemptive way, this was true. On that life-changing sea passage, Patrick began to know the intimate presence of Christ with him in life's storm.

## From Paul's Darkness

Saint Patrick's prayer echoes with familiar strains found in Paul's letter to the believers in Philippi, the very first Christian congregation established in Europe during the first century. Paul, who had weathered his fair share of storms at sea, was now facing a different kind of storm. He wrote to the Philippian believers from Rome, where he was imprisoned and awaiting his sentence. Bound and shackled, at a time when he had most reason to despair, Paul's unshakable confidence, gratitude, joy, and hope in the gospel shone from the darkness of his cell.

In the midst of the darkness, Paul wanted believers to know how to pray. He wanted them to know that in *every* situation, whether the waters were still or raging, they were to raise their voices to God. He exhorts,

> Do not be anxious about anything, but in every situation, by prayer and petition, with thanksgiving, present your requests to God. And the peace of God, which transcends all understanding, will guard your hearts and your minds in Christ Jesus.
>
> Philippians 4:6–7

According to Paul, peace comes through prayer, and most notably when those requests are made in the context of gratitude. Without the context of gratitude, our needs loom exceedingly large, blown to excessive proportions. Gratitude, however, gives us a lens through which to see properly. When we pray with gratitude, God's peace guards our hearts.

Imagine the scene: As Paul wrote these words, he was surrounded by prison walls and armed guards. He knew what it was to be guarded, if not necessarily protected. The city of Philippi was also guarded. In fact, a garrison of Roman soldiers was camped around the city. Stationed on the outskirts throughout each day and night, the job of this battalion was to watch for any enemy forces that might attempt to enter the heart of the city.

As we receive God's promise to guard our hearts and minds in Christ Jesus, the Greek word φρουρέω (*phrouoreo*), or *guard*, can be understood to mean "place a garrison" around your hearts and minds. God protects us with a peace that preserves us from the assaults of anxiety. Isaiah shares this confidence in Isaiah 26:3, "Thou wilt keep him in perfect peace, whose mind is stayed on thee" (KJV). Stephen's fortitude also illustrates this unfathomable peace when he is being stoned to death (Acts 7). He looks to Jesus, and staying his mind on him, he experiences unexplainable, unsurpassable peace.

For Paul, the promise of prayer was not his physical freedom. His prayer from prison was not a request for the storm to stop. Rather, it was a prayer of both thanks and petition. And, against all odds, it was a prayer offered in peace. Writing from his prison cell, Paul was confident of one thing: When believers pray, God's incomprehensible peace comforts them in the storms they face. With the credibility of one who stood in their soggy shoes, Paul conveys his confidence in God's power.

## Prayer in Your Storm

Eighteen centuries later, Ralph Waldo Emerson would echo Paul's insight: "The wise man in the storm prays to God not for safety from danger, but deliverance from fear."

As we're tossed by the waves, God may seem to tarry in quieting the storm, loosing the chains, or healing the disease.

What God *does* do, without fail, is to offer his peace that passes understanding.

Where you find yourself today, whether drifting effortlessly on serene glassy waters or thrown by desperate violent waves, how do your prayers sound? Like sinking Peter, do you instinctively call out to Jesus for help? Or like Jesus' terrified disciples, have you been hesitant to rouse the Master? Hoarse from praying, do you at last offer a humble prayer of relinquishment? Or speechless, desperate, do you simply lift your eyes toward heaven and let the Spirit interpret the groans of your heart?

Know that Jesus' ear is constantly attuned to those who find themselves in life's storms. Sometimes he quiets the storm. Always, he calms and delivers his child.

> Those persons who know the deep peace of God, the unfathomable peace that passeth all understanding, are always men and women of much prayer.
>
> R. A. Torrey

# 3

# Peace in the Hospitable Art of Listening

> Listening is a magnetic and strange thing, a creative force. The friends who listen to us are the ones we move toward. When we are listened to, it creates us, makes us unfold and expand.
>
> Unattributed

Think of the most peaceful homes that you've ever visited or lived in. How did you feel when you walked in the door? Could you sense peace in the air, love on the faces, gentle humor bouncing off walls? Was there a home in your life where, when you entered it, you felt a sigh of relief and surge of contentment? Where you could put up your feet and be yourself, flaws and all, and linger as long as you liked, sharing deeply and laughing into the night? Did the host or hostess greet you with real enthusiasm, and did you feel their good-bye hugs were almost a benediction? My guess is that these homes in your memories or imagination may not have been anything fancy. It may have been littered with toys, books, and newspapers. The food may have been a hot dog and potato chips on a paper plate. But none of these details mattered to you one whit, because when you walked through the door, you entered a place of rest and peace, like Aunt Bea's kitchen on the old black-and-white *Andy Griffith Show*.

Some of us have grandparents' homes in our memories right now; others remember old college friends, simple apartments, and late-night talks; many are blessed enough to think of the homes they grew up in or live in now. Some of us are still dreaming of such a place, wondering if it will ever exist for us. Longing for the reality of feeling truly at home somewhere, or wishing we could provide such a place for others.

A few years ago, I was wandering the four floors of The Tattered Cover bookstore in Denver, when I spotted a spine-out copy of a Henri Nouwen book I had not read. In fact, I had not even heard of the title. I extricated the thin paperback from the over-crowded shelf, noting the subtitle: *The Three Movements of the Spiritual Life*. Only later did I look at the Table of Contents, where the three movements were specified:

"Reaching Out to Our Innermost Self"
"Reaching Out to Our Fellow Human Beings"
"Reaching Out to Our God"

The book is an organized presentation of Nouwen's reflections on the life he has lived. As such, it is intensely personal. It is also intensely practical because it causes me to reflect on my own life with regard to these three most vital relationships. It is one of those books so rich with insight that you want to read a page and then put the book down and take a long walk to reflect on what you have read and how it relates to your world.

I love what Nouwen has to say about solitude and community, what he has to say about prayer and interruptions, but I am especially moved by what he has to say about hospitality:

> Old and New Testament stories not only show how serious our obligation is to welcome the stranger into our home, but they also tell us that guests are carrying precious gifts with them, which they are eager to reveal to the receptive host.[1]

The key word in that sentence is *receptive*. Most of us have full lives, with little margin for lingering with one another. When I am too busy, I find that guests or people or even family members I love become irritants instead of intimates. A friend told me of an insight that came to her after reading Laura Ingall Wilder's *Little House on the Prairie* to her children. "What struck me most," she said, "was how delighted the Ingalls were to have drop-in company. Because the journeys between houses were long, and the harsh winters even longer, visitors were a rare treat. Pa would tap the maple tree, Ma would bake a pie, Pa would get out the fiddle, and there would be a genuine toe-tapping celebration by the hearth. But in my modern life, I'm usually on my way out the door, late for some appointment, and if unexpected company were to just drop by 'for a nice visit' I would be a wreck and probably resent the interruption. Something is wrong with a world where we no longer sit on porch swings and anticipate drop-in, informal chats with neighbors and family." She grew reflective, then added, "What is missing is enough margin in our lives for people, and the peace that comes with being fully present for each other."

How do we practice sharing real hospitality with each other if our lives are always on overload? It is a hard question, and I am not offering easy answers. But I am wondering if we, as

God's peacemakers, should take a good look at the pace of our lives and make adjustments that would create time and space for the spiritual art of hospitality. I wonder what a slowing down of our lives together, in community and in families, would do to improve relationships and our individual well-being. Our fast-forward world of technology is marvelous for many reasons, but I am not sure it is bringing with it much genuine peace.

Nouwen writes,

> Hospitality, therefore, means primarily the creation of a free space where the stranger can enter and become a friend instead of an enemy. Hospitality is not to change people, but to offer them a space where change can take place. . . . Just as we cannot force a plant to grow but can take away the weeds and stones which prevent its development, so we cannot force anyone to such a personal and intimate change of heart, but we can offer the space where such a change can take place.[2]

I've always thought of hospitality as primarily a feminine gift for entertaining, being able to cook meals for people, making them feel welcome in your home, housing them if they need it, and so forth. I never equated it with a way of living your life, of being in the world, as Nouwen did in this passage.

I love that definition of hospitality where we as people begin to see our very selves as homey places to land; where others can fail and grow and learn without force or coercion. Carl Rogers, world-renowned therapist and teacher, said,

> In my early professional years I was asking the question: How can I treat, or cure, or change this person? Now I would phrase the question in this way: How can I provide a relationship which this person may use for his own personal growth?[3]

Whether you live in a welcoming home or a humble apartment, or even out of your car, you can be a living "house" of hospitality by providing the sort of relationship in which another person can relax and grow.

When I think of being a walking, living, breathing form of hospitality, I think of the nearly lost art of deep listening. In his poem "When Someone Deeply Listens to You," John Fox describes the feeling of being deeply heard as "holding up a dented cup you've held since childhood" and having it filled to the brim and beyond with the gift of feeling understood and loved.[4] Kind attentiveness to each other's stories brings uncommon peace between humans.

A friend of mine went with his alcoholic son to a couple of AA meetings, as a guest, and said,

> I wish the church could capture how healing it is to simply listen to one another's stories. In AA you can't 'cross talk' by asking questions or giving advice, which I found really difficult at first. The knee-jerk reaction when someone else is talking is to fill in the spaces with your own words. AA simply provides a safe place for anyone who wants to share, anonymously, and then thanks them for doing so. That's it. Yet this simple form of caring through listening, without pressure to advise or approve, is almost never practiced in homes or churches. I was amazed at the power of it.

Therapists can often sum up what they do by saying, "I help people find their voice, and I hear their stories with the goal to be a kind, non-judging witness. Though I may help and guide, most often it is in the attentive listening itself, simply 'catching and cradling' someone's story, that people begin to get better." When you realize that people pay $150 or more per hour for this service, one has to wonder if people have simply lost the art of lending an ear, friend to friend. Certainly there are times when the strict anonymity and skill of a professional counselor are needed. But there is a wide empty gap of good listeners in our world today. And it seems to me that the best peacemakers I've known have all been highly skilled in the art of deep listening.

Dietrich Bonhoeffer, the beloved Lutheran pastor who was imprisoned and hanged in Germany during the rise of the Nazis, wrote,

> The first service that one owes to others in the fellowship consists in listening to them. Just as love to God begins with listening to His Word, so the beginning of love for the brethren is learning to listen to them. It is God's love for us that He not only gives us His Word but also lends us His ear. So it is His work that we do for our brother when we learn to listen to him. Christians, especially ministers, so often think they must always contribute something when they are in the company of others, that this is the one service they have to render. They forget that listening can be a greater service than speaking.[5]

God doesn't only speak to us through his Word, he "lends us his ear" as he attends to our prayers; he hears us when we talk to him. Philip Yancey wrote,

> Some who attempt prayer never have the sense of anyone listening on the other end. They blame themselves for doing it wrong. . . . Prayer requires the faith to believe that God listens.[6]

The Old Testament is full of references to God hearing our cries, our pleas, our requests. The New Testament only gets bolder. John speaks of the "confidence we have in approaching God: that if we ask anything according to his will, he hears us"

(1 John 5:14). And the writer of Hebrews encourages us to "approach God's throne of grace with confidence [like the beloved child of a King], so that we may receive mercy and find grace to help us in our time of need" (Hebrews 4:16). Therapists use a term to describe the sort of attitude they need to have in their sessions so that people can relax and open up and trust and heal and grow. It is the concept of "unconditional positive regard." The good news is that God invites us to come to him and offers us just such a safe place of unconditional positive regard because he knows we are made of dust and loves us anyway. There is no condemnation because of Christ's sacrifice. There is no fear at all in the sort of love God has, for Jesus came not only to talk and to teach, but to listen to our stories as well. He called the children to him and delighted in their presence. Pointing to the grown-ups gathered around, he said that the entry into the kingdom and its ways is learned by observing these little ones. Children don't know enough to be "impressed"; they are unguarded and open in their trust and requests. Jesus invites us to sit with him a spell and tell him all about everything on our hearts and minds, the way children do when you give them half a chance.

Jesus mingled at parties with saints and sinners, but he seemed to enjoy the company of sinners more. They did not try to impress him, they just told him who they were when he asked, and in his listening, attentive, loving presence they felt both seen and heard. Then their hearts began to melt and their lives changed radically. From tax collectors to the woman caught in adultery, from prostitutes to lepers, it seems he was drawn to the outcasts who had no pride left that could trip them up. God delights in hearing the short, simple prayers like "God have mercy on me," much preferring them over the long, fancy prayers of religious people who are really speaking to impress those around them rather than searching for a heart-to-heart conversation with him.

Peace comes when we know, really know, that God hears us. When we can come running boldly, without fear, into his big office, confident we'll be greeted as his child, with delight in his eyes and a welcoming embrace. There is no business transaction that cannot be halted for a beloved child in need of his Father's ear.

We bring peace to each other when we show hospitality in our homes, yes, but even more so by our very lives and presence. I know of few better ways to do this than to learn and then practice the spiritual art of deep listening. I've often been amazed at how I can go from absolutely frazzled to peaceful after talking to an empathetic friend. How it happens, I don't know. My problems are usually still there, but the angst that was tightly wound around them has relaxed in the listening, caring presence of another human soul. Perhaps this is part of the peace that passes understanding that Paul talks about in his letter to the Philippians. It is a mystery, really, how simply talking to God in prayer (and believing he is listening with love in his eyes), or talking to a friend who cares, brings a measure of peace that cannot be dissected or analyzed. It can only be embraced and gratefully accepted.

> Listen to my words, Lord, consider my lament. Hear my cry for help, my King and my God, for to you I pray. In the morning, Lord, you hear my voice; in the morning I lay my requests before you and wait expectantly.
>
> Psalm 5:1–3

# 4

# Peace Through Friends and Strangers

> The friend who can be silent with us in a moment of despair or confusion, who can stay with us in an hour of grief and bereavement, who can tolerate not knowing . . . not healing, not curing . . . that is a friend who cares.[1]
>
> Henri Nouwen

Red lights flashed and sirens blared. The next thing I knew I was being transported to the ER with heat stroke.

I'd been working outside when I collapsed. I was dehydrated from being out in the sun, and muscles throughout my body were cramping up. Twenty minutes later I was being taken from the ambulance, via stretcher, and wheeled into a space sectioned off by a curtain. There, in the ER, I was given a glucose IV, juice to drink, and a sheet to cover me. I was alone and I was scared.

When the doctor came in to evaluate me, I think he saw the fear in my eyes. He spoke gently, asking me questions about what had happened and how I felt. He was very calm and not hurried at all. And as he talked, he put his hand on my chest. The heat that radiated from his hand warmed me. But more than that, it calmed me and reassured me that I was in good hands. It let me know that he wasn't going anywhere.

Though the episode happened years ago, I have never forgotten that doctor's peaceful, calming presence.

The good doctor's face was, for me, a snapshot of how I imagine Jesus in the boat with his disciples as they were tossed about on the waves. He wasn't the least bit worried. He didn't rush into a frenzy of activity. Rather, his mere presence changed the atmosphere on board. His voice not only calmed the wind and the waves outside the boat, but the wind and the waves within the disciples. I don't know if the doctor who ministered to me was a Christian. I do know, however, that he was used to minister God's calming presence to me in the storm.

Have you experienced God's presence with you through someone else? Maybe you end up sitting next to a stranger at a ball game, or on a subway or an airplane, and the light conversation suddenly dives deeper, and there's an exchange of comfort or empathy or a word of encouragement—exactly what you need at that moment in time. Perhaps, like me, you have encountered peace in a helping professional—a doctor, an ambulance attendant, a therapist. Or maybe it was simply in the arm of a friend, wrapped around your shoulder at just the right time. Often God's chosen vehicle to touch those of us dwelling in mortal bodies is, graciously, the bodies of others.

## Less Than Helpful

Too often, the instinct of many—who sincerely want to help others—is to bark instructions:

> "Hoist the mainsail!"
> "Turn into the wind!"
> "Abandon ship!"

Or they might shout:

> "Eat right!"
> "Exercise!"
> "Take your meds!"
> "Just trust God!"
> "Snap out of it!"

Sometimes, though, what is needed in the storm is someone who is willing to come alongside, to hold, to share tears, and to be comfortable to simply sit in silence. By babbling instructions, we risk making the hurting person feel like a patient being addressed by a doctor who is hurrying off to other tasks. Rather, the calming presence of God is available as we are *received*, just as the intentionally present doctor received me, with the calming presence of Christ himself. That is the kind of person I want to be for others who are being thrashed about by the beating sun and pelting rains. I want to be a calm person, not easily drawn into the fury of another's storm, who can be a solid and stable anchor for the one who suffers.

## Unable to Reach for Help

Whipped by the winds and waves, the very last thing many of us can do in our darkness and despair is to save ourselves. Weary and without strength, we simply cannot hoist ourselves to safety. But in the swirling chaos of our thoughts and fears, when we can no longer stay afloat, some of us are grasped by fellow sojourners (as I was in the face of the good doctor) who have somehow made it to solid ground.

When passengers fled the doomed *Titanic* in lifeboats, some were able to reach across the icy waters and throw a lifeline to other passengers who were desperate and foundering. Working together, they would pull a victim into the safety of the boat, provide a blanket or simply the heat of their own bodies. Once rescued, one could help to rescue another.

In this manner, many have received calm in the storms that threaten to overwhelm. In the faces of friends, or even strangers, they have recognized the palpable presence of God. Someone has lent a listening ear, has reached out with arms of love, bearing God's own presence to one in need.

A family coming home from the hospital following a child's surgery finds a feast set out on their dining room table and a freezer full of prepared meals. A couple facing unemployment, returning home from a day of job searching, finds a generous gift card to the local grocery store tucked into their mailbox. A struggling single mom, raising a teenage son who lives to play basketball, learns that her son has been awarded a full scholarship to summer basketball camp by a mysterious benefactor. When circumstances threaten to undo, others provide tangible signs of God's presence in the midst of the storm.

Sometimes the rescuer will be wearing a cross on a chain

around her neck. Sometimes he will be carrying a Bible. Other times, God sends helpers with no identifying sign other than compassion, and sometimes dressed in the most unusual garb.

## Surprising Sources

One day Jesus entered into a discussion with an expert in the Jewish law who wanted to know how to inherit eternal life. Jesus asked another question: "What is written in the Law?" The man said, "'Love the Lord your God with all your heart and with all your soul and with all your strength and with all your mind; and, Love your neighbor as yourself.'" But the man was in search of a loophole, and so he asked Jesus to define the word *neighbor.* Rather than go into a technical explanation, Jesus offered a story to illustrate. He told about a man on the road to Jericho, who was robbed and beaten by thieves, and left half dead. Along came a couple of "important religious people" who saw the poor soul, but they shifted their eyes away from the sight of trauma and potential trouble, and crossed quickly to the sunnier side of the street. They maintained their outward dignity and piety but did not soil their hands or interrupt their schedules, and ignored a suffering fellow human being.

Then Jesus describes a man who happened to be a Samaritan, a sect of society deemed by Jews to be at the bottom of the religious barrel. Half-breeds viewed as having suspicious historical and theological backgrounds. But this particular Samaritan not only opened his eyes to the hurting man, he walked toward him instead of away from him, his heart full of compassion. The Samaritan personally bandaged the man's wounds, "pouring on oil and wine," then took him to a nearby inn and took care of him. The next day, the Samaritan gave the innkeeper some money (about three days wages) and asked him to look after the man, promising to return and pay the innkeeper more should expenses exceed what he left. Jesus asked, "Which of these three do you think was a neighbor to the man who fell into the hands of robbers?" And the disciples, who knew Jesus and his radical ways pretty well by now, answered, "The one who had mercy on him."

Jesus told them, "Go and do likewise."

In the life of the shipwrecked man, bloodied by the side of the road, God's presence was ministered to him by the most unlikely of rescuers. Jesus says this is how we are to minister as well.

## When We Imitate the Unlikely Rescuer

How do we bring more peace to earth? We drop our religious trappings and pontifications, and enter into the hurt of someone's life with the goal to share a measure of the mercy God has given to us. We get our hands dirty. It generally costs a little time, a little money, and maybe a little pride to be a peacemaker.

How can we be good Samaritans to that person who has fallen among thieves? The thief comes in many forms, with a goal to steal and destroy our perceived value to God. At the beginning of the movie *Platoon,* there is a poignant line: "The first casualty of war is innocence." The thief may be a literal foreign war or a figurative battle that has stolen someone's innocence. The thief may be alcohol or drugs used to numb the pain or to keep the nightmares at bay. The thief may be a disability that you can see, or it may be an inner disability: bipolar disorder, crippling anxiety, chronic depression. Who knows?

What I do know is that Jesus teaches us that when someone crosses our path who is in obvious pain, a true neighbor will not walk away. First you have to look with eyes to see what God sees. How can we love our neighbor if we don't see our neighbor? And how can we see him if we look away, like the priest and the Levite did? If we don't stop, look, and listen, how will we know? And if we don't know, how can we love?

And if we don't love, who in the world are we?

Who have we become . . . or failed to become?

Behind the cardboard sign, the tattoos and piercings, the bankruptcy, the divorce, the public failure . . . is a person. A person with a name and a story. People hear sound bites. God reads the long chapters that lead up to today's headlines, and he knows our unfolding stories. Good Samaritans and peacemakers look *at* people with eyes of mercy, not *through* them with eyes of judgment. They see the bigger picture and never stop praying for a redemptive turn in another's evolving story, no matter how seemingly hopeless. This is the type of care God invites us to extend to others, and it is the surprising gracious care that we receive from the very hand of God.

## Standing Together in Suffering

John and his wife had been married just seven years when breast cancer took her life. The couple had a daughter who was just three years old. In the wake of the traumatic loss, many well-meaning friends and strangers tried to make sense of what made no sense. With the best of intentions, they attempted to shine light into what was, for John, a desperately dark season. Too often, though, their words stung, compounding John's agony:

> "Though you might not understand it now, this is God's good will."
>
> "It was her time. Her work here was through."
>
> "God wanted her with him."
>
> "All things work together for good for those who love God."

So many who meant well only added to John's heavy burden.

One evening after work, John parked in the driveway, freed his daughter from her car seat, gathered their belongings, and headed for the front porch. Unlocking the door to let her inside, he grabbed the day's mail and joined her.

Dropping bags and magazines on the dining room table, he clutched a pile of envelopes. Falling onto the couch, John opened one that was carefully addressed to him in blue ink. Inside the folded note card he read four words:

"We loved her too."

An older Jewish couple from the neighborhood had signed their name below the simple inscription.

For the first time since he'd lost his wife, John felt seen, known, and loved. He received the care of these faithful ones as a gift of peace. He received it as *God's own care* for him.

## A Vision of My Present Helper

When I was a little boy, our family stayed at a cabin in Estes Park, Colorado, one year. During that time my dad took me fishing out on a lake in a small motorboat. After a while, storm clouds rolled in, the temperature dropped suddenly, and it started to rain. The sky quickly grew dark, the wind whipped up, and waves began to slap the sides of the boat. I was clumped in the bow, freezing and afraid, though I didn't say anything.

Seeing me shivering, and seeing how menacing the weather had become, Dad pulled the rope to the outboard motor. It coughed to life, and he headed straight for shore. As he motored us toward safety, I held on for dear life. Our small boat cut through the waves, the bow rising suddenly, then coming down hard on the water, sending a spray of water that felt as though needles were pricking my skin. I had goose bumps on my arms, and my teeth were chattering. Though I had a life jacket on, I didn't know how to swim. I feared being tossed out of the bow and into the dark, deep water. The wind grew stronger, the waves grew higher, and the shore seemed far away.

It was then that I remember turning and looking to where my father stood at the stern, one hand on the rudder as the rain pelted him. I remember the sharp cut of his jaw and how his eyes were set on the shore. He was a strong man and in good shape. I didn't say anything, a pathetic heap of shivering flesh, chilled to the bone. That's when he looked at me with intent eyes that grew suddenly soft and understanding. He smiled. That was all it took. He didn't say anything. He just smiled.

I knew then that we would make it to shore, to our cabin where a warm bath, dry clothes, and hot chocolate would be waiting. I would be safe because my dad was in the stern, his hand on the rudder guiding me home.

Today, whenever I reflect on that moment, I am reminded of the benediction in the book of Numbers, where God used the faces of his priests to make visible the light of his own countenance:

> The LORD bless you, and keep you;
> The LORD make His face shine on you,
> And be gracious to you;
> The LORD lift up His countenance on you,
> And give you peace.
>
> Numbers 6:24–26 NASB

## Help That Truly Helps

God's presence has been made real to me by others who have shown up to be with me. I've discovered that authentic care is different than saying, "Call if you need anything." It's different than offering, "Let me know if I can help." When I'm paddling to stay afloat, I often lack the energy to reach for a phone or even to cry out for help. The ones who've been most helpful to me are those who show up in their work clothes and say, "Put me to work!" Whether it has been cleaning out my refrigerator or mowing my lawn, the tangible expressions of care have kept me afloat when I most needed rescue.

And of course, the ones who know how to be present to me in my suffering aren't always the ones wearing the uniform of a maid or a gardener, an ambulance driver or a doctor. I have just as often been helped when a friend shows up in jeans to say, "Let's go to a movie!" Others have arrived in sneakers and invited, "Let's take a walk." Others, gripping a tennis racket, have knocked on my door and invited me to share a court. Time is a person's most valuable commodity, and when friends have been willing to spend theirs with me, I have been blessed and received God's own grace through them.

## God Provides

During the storms, when we feel the least able to connect to God—to pray, to speak, to listen—we experience God's real presence with us through the faces and hands and voices of both friends and strangers whom he has sent. When living through a devastating divorce, one finds sacred space in the guest room of a colleague from work. When requisite cancer treatments require regular trips to the hospital, another discovers transport from a twenty-one-year-old college student with a flexible schedule. When enduring the loss of a loved one, yet another is handed a packet of Kleenex and a hug in the grocery store. In these precious ones, Jesus himself has stooped to wash our grimy feet.

> Whoever refreshes others will be refreshed.
>
> Proverbs 11:25

# 5

## Peace From God's Word

> In all my perplexities and distresses, the Bible has never failed to give me light and strength.
>
> Robert E. Lee

As a pianist plays "How Great Thou Art," seniors gather in a large public meeting space. Wheelchairs come to rest beside rows of chairs. Walkers are set aside as individuals take their seats. With careful, slow steps, a body gathers to worship. A few family members hold the elbows of loved ones, guiding them toward open seats. Beside her proud grandmother, a teenage girl scans texts on her iPhone as she waits for the service to begin. As an antique clock chimes the hour, a pastor rises and looks out over a sea of gray heads, calling the congregation to worship.

Those gathered in the fellowship area of the assisted living center are a mixed bag of believers. Many are Protestant.

Some are Roman Catholic. A few are curious nonbelievers. At two o'clock on a Sunday afternoon, the worship service is the only option scribbled in on the whiteboard activity calendar. Some have come out of curiosity or boredom. Others, though, have come because worship is what they do. For seventy-four, eighty-one, ninety-six years they have worshiped. And though, for many, memory fails, they continue to present themselves before God in the presence of other believers.

After the pastor calls the congregation to worship, they sing "Amazing Grace." Though some strain to read the font in the blue hymnal left on each chair, more sing from a deep place that seems to circumvent a faulty memory.

As the pianist concludes, congregants who'd carefully risen to their feet, slowly bend to sit again. When the pastor announces that they will join in reading Psalm 23 together, the few who've brought their Bibles flip pages to find the psalm. The pastor begins reading from the King James Version, "The LORD is my shepherd; I shall not want. . . ."

The girl who's come to visit her grandmother lifts her eyes to scan the room. The lips of those with and without Bibles move in synch with the pastor's. Even those women and men whom she knows to be riddled with dementia, unable to participate in the most mundane conversation, come to life as they join the pastor's litany:

> He maketh me to lie down in green pastures: he leadeth me beside the still waters.
> He restoreth my soul: he leadeth me in the paths of righteousness for his name's sake.
> Yea, though I walk through the valley of the shadow of death, I will fear no evil: for thou art with me; thy rod and thy staff they comfort me.

Thou preparest a table before me in the presence of
mine enemies: thou anointest my head with oil; my
cup runneth over.
Surely goodness and mercy shall follow me all the days
of my life: and I will dwell in the house of the LORD
forever.

Psalm 23:1–6 KJV

As the teen girl pauses to look up from her phone, she notices that several faces she knows were wrought with anxiety have softened. Reciting words that have been stored in their bones, she sees that many are experiencing the visceral comfort of Another in the words of Scripture.

## A Reliable Source of Comfort

Many in the room, while enduring physical pain, mental failings, or grief, live daily with loss. In a variety of ways, they experience darkness. And yet, when given the opportunity, these beloved ones experience help where it is most reliably found. They experience real peace and calm from God's Word.

As we weather storms, trying to navigate through the darkness, our temptation is to turn our eyes not toward God's Word, but toward the raging skies. In a storm, we can become so consumed with storm management that we forget to look where help is to be reliably found. In a move that feels almost counterintuitive, as the thunder and lightning threaten, we have confidence that we can expect and receive God's presence through his Word.

We recognize God's help in the stories of God's gracious intervention in the lives of others.

We are reminded of God's presence in the prayers of the psalmist and others.

Through Scripture, we are girded by peace as we witness the Father's faithfulness to his Son Jesus.

In God's Word, we experience calm as we turn our eyes away from the storm and on to the reliable witness of God's faithfulness.

As we allow God's Word to penetrate the deep places of our being, we experience the calming comfort of God's presence with us.

## God's Presence in the Storm

In his letter to the Romans, Paul describes the kinds of whirlwinds we find ourselves in today: We suffer, we live in bondage to decay, and we await redemption. When I have been caught up in a hurricane of circumstances, Paul's exhortation in the eighth chapter of Romans has often calmed me. When my sufferings have loomed large, Paul's words help me gain perspective on the challenges I face.

"If God is for us," asks Paul, "who can be against us?" (Romans 8:31).

Though I know Paul's question is rhetorical, my mind begins to swim with possibilities. A voice inside quickly babbles off a list of those who *can* be against us: creditors, layoffs, broken relationships, enemies, and disease. Paul's list doesn't sound so different from mine. He includes trouble, hardship, persecution, famine, nakedness, danger, and sword. All those *can* be against us! The storms in our lives *can* take our houses, our jobs, our assets, our relationships, our health, and even our lives. But it can't take away the love that God has for us so fully expressed in the sacrifice of his Son.

Ultimately, none, claims Paul, shall defeat us. "In all these things," Paul exhorts, "we are more than conquerors through him who loved us" (Romans 8:37). Paul writes,

> I am convinced that neither death nor life, neither angels nor demons, neither the present nor the future, nor any powers, neither height nor depth, nor anything else in all creation, will be able to separate us from the love of God that is in Christ Jesus our Lord.
>
> Romans 8:37–39

It's comforting to know that God is at work, even when everything else is coming apart. What is of particular comfort to me is what God is doing behind the scenes. The chaos and pain are not for naught! Rather, he is creating a masterpiece out of the pain in our lives. The weight of suffering in my life is lightened because God's Word says that it is not meaningless.

Paul promises, "And we know that in all things God works for the good of those who love him, who have been called according to his purpose" (Romans 8:28). Paul links the hope of this promise to God's deeper purposes, "For those God foreknew he also predestined to be conformed to the image of his Son, that he might be the firstborn among many brothers and sisters" (v. 29). We are predestined to be conformed to the image of Christ! That is the good work he is doing in the midst of all the pain. He is making something of eternal worth. Something that lasts, that can't be taken away from us, no matter what is taken from us in the storm.

This is one of those passages to which I return, again and again when I find myself caught in the winds and the waves.

## Supreme Confidence

A father and son had been swimming in the ocean together when they were pulled out to sea by a riptide. For twelve hours they paddled to stay afloat. When night fell, however, it became difficult for the father to see his son. In the darkness he made up a call-and-response game where he would call out and his son would answer with a playful response. After several hours, however, the son was pulled farther and farther away from his father, and his voice was lost to him. The father was alone. The son was alone.

What is particularly sinister about the storms in our lives is that they feel incredibly isolating. When I begin to feel alone in the storm, I often turn to Psalm 46. There, I am assured, is One who knows what my life is like. Here is Another who has also swum through rough waters.

The psalmist begins by announcing his confidence through the storm:

> God is our refuge and strength, an ever-present help in trouble. Therefore we will not fear, though the earth give way and the mountains fall into the heart of the sea, though its waters roar and foam and the mountains quake with their surging.
>
> Psalm 46:1–3

The psalmist recognizes God's presence in the holy city, in the very midst of the chaos: "Nations are in uproar, kingdoms fall; he lifts his voice, the earth melts" (v. 6).

The entire world is collapsing—physical disasters, military and political chaos. Everything is going to hell in a hand basket. The natural tendency is to run and hide, to fight, to be anxious, to be fearful. To *do* something. The advice of the psalmist is just the opposite:

> He says, "Be still, and know that I am God;
>     I will be exalted among the nations,
>     I will be exalted in the earth."
> The Lord Almighty is with us;
>     the God of Jacob is our fortress.
>
> Psalm 46:10–11

The response is to "Be still, and know that I am God." Military strength isn't our God. Economic strength isn't our God. The collective strength of our national spirit isn't our God. Only he is God—the God of the universe. We are told, essentially, to "relax our grip." We are told to "open our hands." Not to grasp our sword more tightly. Not to hold onto our assets more firmly. "Let go, and let God" is essentially what the psalmist is recommending, as cliché as that may sound. He is our strength, our fortress, our help in time of need. The word *help* is a military term (used also in Psalm 121:1). And it is the fact that we have a covenant relationship with him (the God of Jacob) that we can depend on him to come to our aid, as our ally, and to save us.

Throughout the night, the father who was adrift at sea, separated from his son, assumed his son had drowned. In the darkness, he felt utterly alone. In agony, he prayed to live so that his daughter would not have lost her brother *and* her father, so his wife would not have lost her son *and* her husband in a single tragedy. Graciously, the following day, both the man *and* his son were rescued, separately. Thanks be to God!

The lie of the darkness, which isolates and terrifies, is that we are utterly alone. When we're caught in the storm, blinded by darkness, we are tempted to believe that even God is not with us. Graciously, for the man caught at sea, the lie was dispelled by the light of day. As we turn our hearts to Scripture—to the pages of the Psalms and the Gospels, the patriarchs and letters written by Paul, the prophets and Revelation—we are grounded in the truth of God's presence. In Scripture, the lie that we are alone in the storm is dispelled by the light of truth.

## Encountering a *Person* in Scripture

Currently I am listening to the Gospels on a CD at night and when I wake up in the morning. Specifically, I'm not studying and dissecting them, nor am I seeking to glean a phrase or idea to use in my work, but rather allowing myself to be swept up in the stories. Rather than analyzing them, I am purposing to *inhabit* them.

J. B. Phillips, in his paraphrase of the New Testament, says in his preface that the Word of God is like a bird in flight. Too often we try to analyze the bird instead of craning our necks in awe as it wings its way through the sky. The practical point he makes is that in order to dissect the bird, we first have to capture it, kill it, lay it on the table, cut it open, and pin back the wings as we go into its depths in an attempt to understand it.

And, of course, when we do that, something dies—not simply in the Word, but in us. In our attempt to gain mastery over the mystery, we lose our place in the universe. And maybe that is the root of the fall. We want the knowledge, because knowledge is control. It is power. It is something that can be commoditized, bought and sold.

God doesn't offer his Word as the magic fix-all pill that we can ingest and feel better. Rather, God's Word is the way in which we are invited to encounter the real *person* of God. A. W. Tozer said,

> The modern scientist has lost God amid the wonders of His world; we Christians are in real danger of losing God amid the wonders of His Word. We have almost forgotten that God is a person and, as such, can be cultivated as any person can. It is inherent in personality to be able to know other personalities, but full knowledge of one personality by another cannot be achieved in one encounter.[1]

What I have come to realize is that what I need is a personal encounter with the Savior, not an academic exercise. And I need repeated encounters, as Tozer notes. That happens best, at least for me, when I put myself in the crowd, gathered around the Master Teacher in the Gospels, hearing Jesus for the first time, perhaps, or seeing him for the first time doing a miracle. So often it is said, at the end of such encounters, things like "and the crowd was amazed" or "and everyone was feeling a sense of awe."

The crowds encountered a *person* and they were dazzled by him! I have found that what I need, especially in the storm, is not so much the *written* Word but the incarnate Word. I need his presence so much more than a proof-text or a promise. And so, when I am listening to the Word on a CD, I am trying to imagine the scene, filling in the color and the emotional atmosphere, the sights, the sounds, and trying to stay in the moment, so to speak. All manner of passages in the Scriptures are useful not to the extent that I master them, but to the extent that they lead me to encounter the living *person* of God.

## Where I Have Found Comfort

When Jesus encountered two men on the road to Emmaus who were despondent, he employed passages from the Old Testament to console them, evoking in their minds the promises of God and the memory of his faithfulness.

Passages like these, the ones that comfort me by putting me in touch with the *person* of God include:

> The LORD is close to the brokenhearted and saves those who are crushed in spirit.
>
> Psalm 34:18

> I will fear no evil, for *you are with me.*
>
> Psalm 23:4 (emphasis mine)

> And surely I am with you always, to the very end of the age.
>
> Matthew 28:20

> Never will I leave you; never will I forsake you.
>
> Hebrews 13:5

> The Word became flesh and blood, and *moved into the neighborhood.*
>
> John 1:14 THE MESSAGE (emphasis mine).

I also encounter the *person* of Jesus in Mark's telling of Jesus' disciples banding together against the gales of a storm. Jesus has pulled away from the crowds to be with his Father, sending his disciples across the lake in a boat. When he sees them struggling, he walks out onto the water. Thinking Jesus is a ghost, they cry out in terror.

Jesus' words of comfort to his disciples? "Take courage; it is I, do not be afraid." And I love the verse right after that: "Then He got into the boat with them, and the wind stopped; and they were utterly astonished" (Mark 6:51 NASB).

I love that Jesus went out onto the sea, in the dark of night, in the midst of the storm. It wasn't the disciples looking for Jesus, but Jesus looking for the disciples. He didn't call to them from the safety of the shore; he put himself in *their* storm. And came to *their* boat. Which to me is the message of the incarnation (see Matthew 1:23, "And they shall call His name Immanuel, which translated means, 'God with us'" NASB).

As you turn to the Scriptures for hope and comfort, *Immanuel* is the one you seek. There is no comfort to be found in words for the words' sake. But those that point you to the living presence of God with you will buoy you in the storm.

## Where to Turn

When you're being tossed about by the waves, when you reach for the Scriptures during the storm, do you know where to turn for comfort?

If God has been steering the rudder of your ship throughout your lifetime, if you have a rich history of nesting yourself deep within the pages of the Bible, you may know *exactly* where to turn to find God's soothing presence. Perhaps the binding of your Bible is bent wide open at Psalm 23. Dog-eared pages may mark Isaiah 43 as the place where you dock during storms. Personally penned notes in the index may send you to Matthew 11:28.

Should you be newer to placing your trust in God, or just beginning to anchor yourself in his Word, the thick Bible that sits atop your bedside table may seem intimidating. Perhaps you've purposed to read it cover to cover, only to get mired in a swamp of genealogies or ancient commandments. Because the Bible is a compilation of many forms of literature, assembled across many years of history, representing many unique voices, it's no surprise that some feel lost. Perhaps you know others who gain rich strength from God's Word, but you've not yet been able to access its treasures.

Be gentle with yourself.

I suggest that as you search the Scriptures for the peace that God promises, you consider beginning in the Psalms. If you crack open your Bible in the center of the book, you're likely to land on a psalm. The Psalter, a collection of 150 poetic prayers, many originally sung, has been called both the prayer book and the hymnal of the church. Some of these are songs of praise, celebrating God's goodness and mercy. Some of the prayers are desperate pleas for help from those who are sinking. Some are prayers of confession, admitting to God how unclean our hearts are.

In the prayerful pages of the Psalms, you will encounter the company of sailors just like yourself, with their eyes open to recognize God's presence during the darkest of nights. Don't try to plow your way through the Psalms in a week or even a month. Rather, let yourself soak in each one like a warm bath. Settle into a single psalm for a week or so. Let it speak to you. Converse with it. Let it form you. Read it aloud. Memorize the verses that have captured your heart. Most of all, let it minister to you the *real presence* of the God who is with you and for you.

Beloved, God longs to bathe you with the warmth of his calming presence. One of the most reliable ways to encounter and experience God's peace is through the pages of his Word.

Soak it in.

> Great peace have those who love your law, and nothing can make them stumble.
>
> Psalm 119:165

# 6

# Peace in and Through Music

In a world of peace and love, music would be the universal language.[1]

Henry David Thoreau

Gavin Bryars is a brilliant eclectic British composer, most famous for two creative compositions: "The Sinking of the Titanic" and "Jesus' Blood Never Failed Me Yet." The latter work has moved people to deep emotion and tears (even those who have no religious leanings), and often they are at a loss for explaining why. In an interview, Gavin Bryars explained how this unique, touching musical piece came into being. He was living in London at the time, working on the soundtrack for a friend's film about Londoners living on the frayed hem of the city. They were drunks and down-and-outers mostly, and as this ragged group was being filmed, some would suddenly and unexpectedly burst into song. The songs were often slurred, sentimental renditions of better times, better bars, better whiskey. But one of the men, who wasn't drunk, who in fact didn't drink, sang a different song. It was a simple song of faith: "Jesus' Blood Never Failed Me Yet."

> When I played it at home, I found that his singing was in tune with my piano, and I improvised a simple accompaniment. I noticed, too, that the first section of the song—thirteen bars in length—formed an effective loop that repeated in a slightly unpredictable way. I took the tape loop to Leicester, where I was working in the Fine Arts Department, and copied the loop onto a continuous reel of tape, thinking about perhaps adding an orchestrated accompaniment to it. The door of the recording room opened to one of the large painting studios, and I left the tape copying, with the door open, while I went to have a cup of coffee. When I came back, I found the normally lively room unnaturally subdued. People were moving about much more slowly than usual and a few were sitting alone, quietly weeping.
>
> I was puzzled until I realized that the tape was still playing and that they had been overcome by the old man's singing. This convinced me of the emotional power of the music and of the possibilities offered by adding a simple, though gradually evolving, orchestral accompaniment that respected the tramp's nobility and simple faith. Although he died before he could hear what I had done with his singing, the piece remains as an eloquent, but understated testimony to his spirit and optimism.[2]

Since the first notes from human voices were sung, the first sounds of crude instruments played, music has been a direct line to the soul's deepest emotions, seemingly bypassing the brain altogether at times.

There are so many moments in life when words fail, and only music can express what our soul struggles to say. I'm sure you could share the music that has serenaded the happiest moments of your life, motivated you to wake up or work out, and comforted you through life's storms.

When you think of pure joy or happiness, what songs bounce around in your brain?

What song gets you moving when you need a push to work out, accomplish a big goal, or start all over again after being knocked down? (Really, can any of us hear "The Eye of the Tiger" without wanting to run up a hundred steps with the energy of Rocky Balboa? Pretty much the ultimate "Get 'er done" song.)

What are your go-to pieces of music when you need comforting and an infusion of peace for your hurting soul?

Soundtracks, like the one from *Shadowlands,* comfort me. Anything by Mark Isham—*Life as a House, A River Runs Through It*, has a calming effect in restless times.

I visited a woman in a hospice facility whose baby was dying. She would curl up in bed every night with him, just to be near and hear him breathe. The malady is unimportant; she knew his time on earth would be brief. The sadness was, at times, more overwhelming than she could bear. *The Seal Lullaby* by Eric Whitacre and his choir is about a mother seal singing to its pup. The lyrics are beautiful, so evocative, so serene. Since then, every time I listen to it, I think of this family and pray for them. It gives me peace somehow.

Henryk Gorecki's *Symphony of Sorrows* has been mysteriously comforting to me in disorienting times. Luciano Pavarotti singing "Nessun Dorma" makes me long for the Lord's return and almost always brings tears to my eyes, and after the tears, peace.

One of the most beautiful and soothing musical discoveries for me is from an orchestral–choral album by Jonathan Elias, *The Prayer Cycle*. About halfway through the gorgeous instrumental, James Taylor's folksy familiar voice enters, singing of being in a very small boat in a large sea, and like a lost little boy, he sings for his Father to carry him home. If you are in a place of feeling lost and alone, too overwhelmed even to find the words to explain it, Google this piece, and let it become your prayer. Let it wash peace over your soul.

## Music Transports Us

Have you ever been driving along, minding your own business, and heard a song that suddenly took you to another place, another time, another person . . . so that you almost forgot where you were or what you were doing? A friend of mine told of driving past her children's school while listening to Pachelbel's "Canon in D." She was transported, in her mind, to the beautiful memory of her sister walking down the aisle in her wedding dress to this gorgeous piece of music. "I was so in the moment, that I could see the smile on my sister's lovely veil-framed face, the sun through the stained-glass windows, my cute kids trailing behind her as flower girl and ring-bearers. I 'came to' in the next town, not realizing that I'd been driving for twenty miles past my destination."

## Music in Scripture

The Bible is riddled with music and song, and in fact, sandwiched by song. The first song mentioned in Scripture is from

Exodus, chapter 15; the last song is in Revelation 15. The first is sung by the children of Israel as they are led to freedom out of Egypt's slavery. The last? Fascinatingly, it is also a refrain of the ancient "Song of Moses" coupled with a new song, "The Song of the Lamb." Both songs of freedom after long, dark seasons of slavery, are woven together in one majestic musical moment to end all moments.

David the shepherd boy was called in to the royal court and asked to play his harp to soothe the savage beast of raging emotions in King Saul. This same David composed dozens of songs, originally meant to be sung and played, though we call them psalms and read them like prose. Even so, the Psalms remain the most worn pages in most Bibles because the lyrical words read like poetry and touch us, honestly and deeply, in times of both struggle and joy. We don't turn to a teaching epistle when we are going through the worst of times; we dive for the twenty-third Psalm and the imagery that soothes our souls, to green pastures and cool waters on the other side of the valley of the shadow of death. Music lyrics and poetry bring peace in ways nothing else can. They are gifts from heaven to help ease the pain of being human.

Singing angels in the night sky heralded the good tidings of great joy, announcing the coming of our Savior, our Prince of Peace, God-in-the-flesh. God himself created and uses music to punctuate what matters most.

## Music Expresses What Words Alone Cannot

Corrie ten Boom was sort of sleep-walking in disbelief, unable to express the flood of emotions she'd kept at bay during the torturous years she spent in a Nazi prison camp. She was now in a hospital filled with friendly, caring nurses and other medical staff. In her book *Tramp for the Lord*, she wrote, "Far in the distance I heard the sound of a choir singing, and then, oh, joy, the chimes of a carillon. I closed my eyes and tears wet my pillow. Only to those who have been in prison does freedom have such great meaning."

> Later that afternoon one of the nurses took me up to her room where for the first time in many months I heard the sound of a radio. Gunther Ramin was playing a Bach trio. The organ tones flowed about and enveloped me. I sat on the floor and sobbed unashamedly. It was too much joy. I had rarely cried during all those months of suffering. Now I could not control myself. My life had been given back as a gift. Harmony, beauty, colors, and music.[3]

How fitting that Corrie's exit from "hell" to a place of peace was accompanied by the strains of Bach. The music, mingled with her grateful tears, said more than any spoken prayer could express.

Sometimes music brings peace in times of unspeakable joy. It also brings calm in times of unimaginable sorrow.

The RMS *Titanic* was not only the pride of the White Star Line, it was the pride of the Edwardian Era, where man was triumphing over nature in every area, from medicine to technology. Like the builders of the Tower of Babel, man was ascending into the heavens, and in the process, making a name for himself.

This pride presaged its fall, or in this case, its sinking.

In the early morning hours of April 14, 1912, sometime after the collision with an iceberg, the band came on deck to calm the passengers with music. The first song they played was

"Ragtime." There was still hope for rescue at this point, and a song with a happy beat kept spirits up.

Shortly before the ship sank, though, when they realized that their SOS wasn't going to be answered, the band changed its tune to what was a collective prayer. The last song they played was "Nearer My God to Thee."

## Music Eases the Way Into Birth and Death

Young mothers today labor and give birth to music they've prerecorded on their playlists. They tell me that music brings a measure of peace, and for many, eases some of the pain of childbirth. They pick out special songs to be played for their newborn as he takes his first breath, and hears his first sounds. The presence of music increases their joy. In one study, "Brahms' Lullaby" was prescribed for premature infants as part of an experiment. The babies gained weight faster and went home a week earlier than infants who did not hear the lullaby.

Further down the hospital halls, in sick units and hospice rooms, you can also find music playing, bringing peace at the other end of life. After the two World Wars, volunteers at Veterans hospitals began to play music and sing for patients. Patient response was so positive, stimulating good healing reactions, that hospitals began hiring musicians. In one hospital, they found that half an hour of listening to music had the same effect as ten milligrams of Valium. Patients who had not been able to fall asleep for as long as three or four days, fell into a peaceful sleep listening to music. ("Take two arias and call me in the morning"?)

Today, in many hospitals and hospices, a family can arrange for a couple of specially trained musicians to sing or play live music, a "music vigil," for someone who is dying. The private concert usually lasts about an hour. This is of special comfort during the hours before death or when life support is removed, both to the patient and to his loved ones. The presence of music brings peace and comfort in times of sorrow, transitions, and disorientation.

## Sharing Peace Through Music

When I want to comfort a friend who is hurting, my first instinct is to share with them what has comforted me. Often that turns out to be a piece of music that has ministered to my heart during a rough patch. When a dear friend of mine went through a tough week, her alcohol-addicted son pouring hot coals of profanity and cruelty on her tender heart in a booze-induced rage, I wanted to remind her how precious she is to the Lord, to me, and so many others. To somehow replace her son's verbal poison with life-lifting nourishment. But how? In the end, I gave her a gift bag with a devotional Bible, a bottle of good red wine, and the soundtrack from the movie *Somewhere in Time,* one of my own go-to CDs for soul-soothing comfort.

She thanked me and later described sitting down for a good meal, sharing the wine with her husband, the music providing a background of much needed respite and beauty. She said, "It was one of the most thoughtful gifts I've ever received. You gave my assaulted brain an hour of healing serenity."

Who among us couldn't use an hour of healing serenity? Even ten minutes could change the mood of your day. Whether you need Ragtime, Bach, or some '70s Rock, let the gift of music bring you a dose of peace. Sing along if you feel like belting one out. An old hymn says it so well: "Sometimes a light surprises the Christian while he sings; it is the Lord who rises with healing in His wings."[4]

> The Lord your God is with you. . . . He will take great delight in you; in his love he will no longer rebuke you, but will rejoice over you with singing.
>
> Zephaniah 3:17

# 7

# Peace Through Deep Rest

> Because we do not rest, we lose our way. . . . We miss the compass points that would show us where to go; we bypass the nourishment that would give us succor. We miss the quiet that would give us wisdom. We miss the joy and love born of effortless delight. Poisoned by this hypnotic belief that good things come only through unceasing determination and tireless effort, we can never truly rest.[1]
>
> Wayne Muller

One of the most touching scenes from the beloved movie *Fiddler on the Roof* opens with five coming-of-age daughters and their mother busily setting the Sabbath table with their best dishes. In the center of the table are two loaves of challah bread (symbolizing manna) covered with a traditional embroidered cloth. The family and two guests are hurrying about, washing up, changing into their finest clothes. At the edges of the table scene,

Golda, the high-strung Jewish wife and mother, is nagging her husband Tevye, who avoids her constant pressuring by humming prayers, silently indicating he is busy talking to God. In another room of the simple kosher home, one daughter urges a poor young tailor to ask her father for her hand in marriage this very night. The tailor is a jumble of new love and frazzled nerves. As the household moves to take their places around the table, there are glances between the family and guests—some fervent, some suspicious, some worried, some irritated—the everyday stuff of family drama.

Golda places a lace veil over her head, and Tevye trades his cloth cap for a yarmulke. It is eighteen minutes before sundown, and as the family gathers around the table, there is a pause, then silence, a collective sign of . . . letting go. Golda's frantic countenance relaxes as she looks her husband full in the face. He returns her gaze with his own eyes of love. In this place of grace, they remember who they are to each other, at the core, beneath the fussing and nagging and avoiding. Golda lights the candles and waves her hands above the flames toward her, three times, symbolizing a taking in of light and of the essence of *Shabbat,* which means "rest." Peace begins to descend, troubles and worries and irritations flee as the mama and papa invite God's peace into their home, invoking his blessings on the head of each child. From this moment of sundown on Friday evening until three stars appear in the sky on Saturday, the family will rest from their work and their busyness, as a way to acknowledge that God is in charge of their lives and they are not. "When we cease interfering in the world," writes Lauren Winner in *Mudhouse Sabbath,* "we are acknowledging that it is God's world."[2]

Though it is not portrayed in the movie scene, Jewish custom is that the father will also sing a special blessing of honor over his wife while standing behind her, touching her shoulders, reminding the family of her great worth to the home. "At some Shabbat tables, when the challah is blessed, each person touches the challah, or touches someone who is touching the challah, so that everyone is connected to that which nourishes and sustains—food, family, and love."[3] Though there will be no work or business conducted, there will be great food, good wine and good conversation, and for husbands and wives . . . later that evening, in the privacy of their marriage bed, there will be lovemaking.

In the film, toward the end of the singing of the Sabbath prayer, the camera pans to other homes, other Jewish mothers waving their hands above the candles (one symbolizing the word *keep* and the other the word *remember*), and then widens to a view of the entire village, candlelight glowing in each and every home as the sun sets on the horizon. Shabbat is for the refreshment of marriages, for families, and indeed for the whole community of God.

It is for *you*.

"The Sabbath was made for man," said Jesus, who called himself the Lord even of the Sabbath, "not man for the Sabbath" (Mark 2:27). God gave us the Sabbath because he knew we would never rest from our worries and squabbles and labors unless he put a symbolic STOP sign in front of his ever-wandering, weary children. A sign that says, in essence: STOP. BREATHE. CELEBRATE. REST. To adapt a phrase from a milk advertisement, "Sabbath does a body good."

"Shabbat is like nothing else. Time as we know it does not exist for those twenty–four hours, and the worries of the week soon fall away. A feeling of joy appears. The smallest object, a leaf or a spoon shimmers in a soft light, and the heart opens. Shabbat is a meditation of unbelievable beauty."[4]

It is enough to make one wish to have been born Jewish, avoiding of course, the heavy trials that have been Israel's lot through the centuries. There's a song of uniquely Jewish humor on the Internet, summing up their history in one succinct sentence: "They tried to kill us; we survived, let's eat!"

At the end of a typical work and drama-filled week, wouldn't it be wonderful to look forward to a candle-lit evening, a good meal, family and friends, wine, and a universal agreement to set aside differences and focus on the Lord's blessings? The world, in its own way, takes its toll on us, often defeating and discouraging us. But with Sabbath awareness of the One who is really in charge, we survive. Clink the goblets. *L'Chaim!* To life! Let's eat.

## Jesus, Our Source of Peaceful Rest

In one of Christ's last interchanges with his disciples before setting his face toward the cross, Jesus took the opportunity to speak to them, lovingly and intimately, saying,

> Come to me, all you who are weary and burdened, and I will give you rest. Take my yoke upon you and learn from me, for I am gentle and humble in heart, and you will find rest for your souls.
>
> Matthew 11:28–30

Have you ever noticed how the most poignant and important, tender and loving things between friends and family members are often said just before the good-byes? Mothers ruffle the hair of the daughters and kiss the cheeks of their grandbabies with tears in their eyes, wordlessly verbalizing affection. Fathers and sons, who may have been teasing or sparring through the day, wrap each other in a bear hug and exchange an "I love you" or "I'm proud of you" at front doors and car doors in a parting scene repeated in generation after generation.

In a prayer a few verses before the conversation of Matthew 11:28–30, Jesus had tenderly referred to the disciples as "little children." You can almost see the Savior make a shift from acting as teacher to a more paternal role. He knows his time on earth is coming to a close, and now he shuts his lesson planner, looks up into the eyes of his beloved friends, and spends a little time speaking from his heart to theirs. The parting topic on his mind is the gift of deep rest.

He says to them, "Come unto me, all you who are weary and burdened . . ." And in that phrase "Come unto me" is expressed deep love and compassion.

When someone you care about is obviously tired and worried as they stumble in the front door of your home, and you say, "Come here . . ." what are you implying you will give? Most of us immediately imagine a welcoming, comforting hug. Jesus last uttered the words "Come unto me" to small children, inviting them—against the wishes of the grown-ups—to come to him and climb onto his lap and be held in his arms. He extends the same invitation to us, for inside aren't most of us still about six years old, legs dangling from a tall chair, confused and wondering what in the world is going on?

Christian speaker and writer Sandra Aldrich, a Kentucky mother from the South with a personality as big as all outdoors, invites stressed-out souls to lay their burdens down when they enter her home. She greets them with "Haul it on in here, honey," and then gives them a mug of something warm to drink and an hour or two of nurturing mingled with focused listening. People leave her modest home feeling lighter, their brows unfurrowed, and rested in soul and body. This is the Savior's personal invitation to our tired, worn-out selves, when we simply come to him with our burdens, "hauling it all in" to him. He promises us what we all long for: true rest.

He actually offers two kinds of rest, and all in this one passage.

The first rest he promises is the very practical physical and mental rest that comes from connecting with someone who replenishes us in times of physical exhaustion or emotional stress. It is the same Greek word used to describe the hospitality of Onesimus, who visited and encouraged Paul when he was in prison, "refreshing" him (bringing him rest). In the simple presence of someone who cares, we can put our emotional feet up, exhale, and be at ease.

A friend of mine talked of living in a long, painful marriage with a husband who was eventually diagnosed with narcissistic personality disorder. This meant that he never looked at his wife with compassion, never listened but only debated, never paused to comfort her soul, only to challenge her thoughts and motives at every turn. He was always searching for an angle, forcing all communication into a game where he needed to land on top and win, and needed her to be "less than" and lose. His life goal seemed to be to keep her humble, to break her down.

It exhausted her to the core of her soul.

"We went to a marriage counselor," my friend shared one day. "And the kind counselor, a fatherly man, saw the pain in my eyes, the tears streaming down my face, and his own eyes grew soft as he compassionately said, 'Oh my. There's a lot of pain here.'

"With those few simple, caring words, I relaxed and began to feel safe. This kind man *saw* me. He didn't look through me for an argument or a point to debate, but his eyes simply and gently settled on mine. How long had it been since a man, other than my father, had shown me deep caring? It reminded me of the phrase from 'O Holy Night': *'Then he appeared, and the soul felt its worth.'* In this safe, compassionate therapist's presence, I felt my worth slowly returning. My feelings mattered. My brokenheartedness invoked a caring response instead of judgment. This was the first real glimmer of value and peace I'd felt in years."

The Shepherd is good, Jesus says of himself, because he knows and cares for his sheep. He welcomes them and creates a place of ultimate safety. He guides them to cool waters and green pastures. And shows them when it is time to pause and rest.[5]

## Slumbering Rest

If we are honest, there are days when our minds are not places where anyone should go alone. There are days when our inner world feels "formless and empty," a place of darkness and churning, without going anywhere or accomplishing anything of value. Much the way the earth is described in Genesis 1:1. The exhausted brains through which we view the world, others, and even God, has a dark and foggy lens, full of inaccuracies and negativity, ambivalence and apathy.

In short, as they say in West Texas, "It ain't purty."

The prescription for irritation and being overwhelmed may not be as complicated as getting your brain balanced, seeing a doctor or therapist, or engaging a spiritual director. It could be as simple as taking a nice guilt-free nap!

We can invoke the Creator to hover over the mess that is often our minds, and ask him to bring order out of the chaos. Shine his light on the darkness. Create fresh thoughts, perspectives, ideas, and illumination. God's gift of sleep re-boots our bodies and minds, not unlike an overwhelmed computer that begins to work again after it is allowed to shut down awhile for internal repairs. Part of being human is that we need rest the way we need air and food and love to be of any use to anyone. We are cranky toddlers in five- or six-foot bodies, demanding and disoriented. All many of us need is our blankey and bed and a good-night prayer to have our sanity restored.

Whether we are taking a short power nap, having a good night's sleep, a real vacation, or a day off, "sabbathing" of all lengths and varieties is part of God's provision in a balanced and peaceful life. In truth, sleep may be the most spiritual discipline some of us can begin to employ.

## Rest for Your Souls

Jesus continues his offer of rest with a second thought: "Take my yoke upon you and learn from me, for I am gentle and humble in heart, and you will find rest for your souls" (Matthew 11:29).

This second word for "rest" is a spiritual place (under his yoke) that the Savior longs for us to find and then learn to abide in. In other words, he wants us to settle down and make our home in the comfort that he is approachable, safe, "gentle and humble in heart." The more you learn of Christ's ways, the more you'll discover that he is the most down-to-earth God of the Galaxies you'll ever relax with.

The yoke Jesus asks us to share with him he says is easy. And the burden is light. In biblical times, farmers trained young oxen by yoking or harnessing them together with an older, stronger ox. They would even soften the young ox's yoke by padding it with soft cloth. And here's the most interesting fact: The younger ox would not actually pull the load. That was the job of the elder ox. The younger ox simply walked alongside the older one, yoked together but not shouldering the burden.

I cannot help but wonder if this is the ultimate picture of the "soul rest" Jesus had in mind. *The Message* paraphrases the words of Jesus in a beautiful way: "Take a real rest. Walk with me and work with me—watch how I do it. Learn the unforced rhythms of grace. I won't lay anything heavy or ill-fitting on you. Keep company with me and you'll learn to live freely and lightly" (11:29–30).

Walking and working together with Christ, in natural, unforced rhythms of grace. What a profoundly peaceful way to be in the world.

## Choosing Rest, Choosing Peace

In every way, on every front, through every storm and crazy trial, the Lord of the Sabbath, the Prince of Peace, the Good Shepherd, woos us to take a real rest. Even when we are working, there's a choice: We can work in angst or we can yoke up with Jesus, letting him shoulder the heavy stuff that is weighing us down. We can work alongside him in a state of relaxed peace. Maybe we won't get there overnight, but as we learn more and more of his gentle and humble nature, rest for our bodies and souls will come.

Where could you add more Sabbath and less stress to your days? Can you pause a time or two this very day to reflect on the Lord's goodness? Or perhaps all you need is a good nap or a peaceful night's sleep, allowing the Creator to restore order from chaos while you let go and trust him. Maybe you need to shift the heavy burdens you were not created to carry over to the strong shoulders of the Savior. Or perhaps you are drawn to metaphorically (or physically) light a candle, wave the light of shalom peace toward your face. Put aside the laptop, smartphone, spreadsheet, or to-do list, and look deeply into the eyes of the people you love; say a prayer of blessing and gratitude, eat a meal in a beautiful setting, raise a glass and toast this brief, beautiful life while you have the gift of breath to do so.

"I am leaving you with a gift—peace of mind and heart," Jesus said in his parting words, in his newly resurrected body. "And the peace I give is a gift the world cannot give. So don't be troubled or afraid" (John 14:27 NLT).

> His rest, his peace, his calm, his serenity.
> All yours. All mine.
> Any day, any time.
> All you have to do is come to him like a tired child, in utter trust.
> He will take over from there.
> It is as hard, and as easy, as this.
> *Shalom.*[6]

> O LORD, you have examined my heart and know everything about me. You know when I sit down or stand up. You know my thoughts even when I'm far away. You see me when I travel and when I rest at home. You know everything I do.
>
> Psalm 139:1–3 NLT

# 8

# Peace Through the Body of Christ

> What does love look like? It has the hands to help others. It has the feet to hasten to the poor and needy. It has eyes to see misery and want. It has the ears to hear the sighs and sorrows of men. That is what love looks like.[1]
>
> Augustine

Christ's presence in our lives often seems elusive, a bit like his appearances after the resurrection, where he draws near, then suddenly is gone. At times it seems a parlor trick of some celestial sort. He is walking with the two grieving followers on the road to Emmaus, then in the second it takes to break a loaf of bread he's no longer with them. He materializes in a room, shows himself to the disciples, then vanishes into thin air. And finally, like an act of levitation, he ascends into the clouds as his disciples watch, mystified. His presence seems inconsistent, yet we are told that he will never leave or forsake us, that he will be with us unto the ends of the earth.

Like the popular search-and-find children's book *Where's Waldo?*—we look for Jesus in the multitude of pressures, needs, to-do lists, painful thoughts, or disorienting circumstances of our lives.

Most of us have experienced calling out to God in a moment of despair and agony, the storms of discouragement or shock reeling about us, only to feel God's echoing silence. *Maybe he's lost my file.*

We've all known people who claim to have had close encounters of the God kind, where Jesus comes to them in a dream or a vision or handwriting on their iPad, but most of the time, Christ limits himself to showing up via his most common, chosen vessel of spiritual communication: the body of Christ. He comes through someone who is praying, being attentive, listening to the Word or the promptings of the Holy Spirit. Perhaps in a moment of deep struggle, you've received a call from a friend saying, "You've been on my mind all day. How are you?" When yielded to Christ, we become each other's angels unawares in feet of clay.

It's more than a little humbling, and often frightening, to realize that Christ's church, namely you and me, is commissioned to be God-with-skin-on to the world and to one another for the duration on this planet. It's almost laughable. I picture an adult handing over the keys to a Lexus to their twelve-year-old kid who struggles to make his bed and turn in his homework on time. What was Jesus thinking? Honestly, most of us are so self-absorbed in our own little dramas and traumas, we rarely look up and about us with a heart to serve someone else. It seems to me that as a whole, we humans, even the most faithful among us, should not be trusted with a mission of this magnitude. That God chose to put such a divine task into our clumsy, earthy hands is beyond remarkable.

Yet the crazy truth of it is, we are called to be his love, his calm, his peace. We are to be his eyes and his hands to one another.

And when by some wild miracle we actually do show up for each other in the body of Christ, it is a beautiful thing to behold. We become his living peace on earth, his breathing goodwill to men. In the feeding of the five thousand, it was clear that Jesus was happy to equip the disciples to do what needed to be done. But there were limits to what he was willing to do. Jesus didn't wiggle his nose and make a nice hot plate of fish and bread appear in front of each person gathered on that crowded hillside. The disciples took the meager meal they had found, offered it to Jesus to bless and multiply, then handed out the gift *themselves* to God's hungry children. In essence, they became Christ's feet and hands as they distributed his miracle of multiplied food.

Time and again, Jesus will take whatever ridiculously small talents we have to give him, and as we simply show up with a willing heart, he blesses and multiplies the offering. We are God's chosen vessels to get it done. He is not going to "zap the world right" through some magic trick. At least not until the day of his return. Ready or not, for better or worse, we're *it*. We, God's children in blue jeans and Dockers, with packed calendars, too-small bank accounts, and overwhelmed brains, are the closest thing to God's superheroes on earth. So we must sometimes put aside our self-absorption and agendas, let the Holy Spirit fill these imperfect vessels, and be willing to move among people, look into their eyes, and give them something to fill their stomachs or their souls, their loneliness or their confusion, or even their empty pockets. We are called to be his peacemakers, and when we answer the call, we often find ourselves feeling calmed as well, reminded of the Father's tender care for us all. "Blessed are the peacemakers," Jesus said, "for they will be called children of God" (Matthew 5:9).

You'll recall that after the disciples gave out thousands of fish and loaves of bread, they each had a basket full of their own to take home. This is the way kingdom magic works. We show up to serve, and later we find ourselves walking away with a surprise basket of goodies: We too are strangely filled and blessed. Scientists call it the "helper's high," social researchers find that people who live a rich life of service live longer and are happier than others. It seems we are wired for reaching out to other human beings. To show up and care when we can with whatever we have to offer.

## Made for This

When we give what we have to offer, we are entering into the life patterned for us by Jesus himself.

Before his crucifixion, storm clouds were gathering over the disciples. Though they'd noticed the winds had increased around Jesus, that the sun was hidden behind a cloud, they still weren't able to predict the magnitude of what was brewing. Jesus, however, understood. He foresaw the darkness that was coming, and what he most wanted to do was to prepare his friends, to gird them to weather the storm ahead.

After sharing a meal together, he surprised them by taking off his outer clothing and wrapping a servant's towel around his waist. Then filling a pitcher with water, he stooped to wash the disciples' dusty feet. This radical act of love, a master bending to serve his students in this most humble task, was nothing less than scandalous. Immediately Peter resisted. At Jesus' firm insistence, however, he relented, allowing his feet to be washed. Kneeling, pouring water over his friend's feet, Jesus gently cleansed away the filth of the road. One by one, the other disciples received the same tender, intimate care.

Standing to face the Twelve, Jesus gave meaning to the moment, explaining, "Now that I, your Lord and Teacher, have washed your feet, you also should wash one another's feet. I have set you an example that you should do as I have done for you" (John 13:14–15). The pattern, he was explaining, is this: You are to love each other as I have loved you. Not wanting to leave the word *love* open for interpretation—lest it be confused with how they already understood *Master* or *Teacher* or *Lord*—he modeled for his followers a love that stooped to serve. This was to become the pattern for their lives together. Specifically, the strong would bow in service to the weak.

Following Jesus' resurrection and ascension, as the earliest followers of Jesus figured out together how they were to love one another, their life was marked by that love. Like the passengers of the *Titanic* who'd been rescued by those already in lifeboats, the body of Christ extended an arm to those in need. When widows were hungry, the community fed them. When some had plenty, they shared with those in want. Working together, the body of Christ stayed afloat in the storm and were an example to the world.

## Whose Footprints?

A popular story of God's care in the storm elicits, for me, a visual image of God's care being extended in this way through the hands and feet and faces of his body. The story is told of a man who had a dream of walking along the beach with God. In it, the scenes from his life flash across the sky. As they do, he notices two sets of footprints in the sand, one set his and the other God's. Looking back at the footprints in the sand, he noticed that at the lowest points in his life there was just one set of footprints. Disappointed, he wondered why, when life was the most cruel, it appeared God had left him.

During the storms of our lives, it can feel as though we've been left alone. We feel abandoned. Forsaken. Through the pounding rains we become unable to recognize God's promised presence. During the lowest points in my own life, I've wanted to ask God the same question! Where were you when I stumbled? Where were you when I cried? Where were you when I suffered? And where are you now?

Bothered, the man walking on the beach, wondering the same, asked God about the conspicuous absence. Gently, the Lord replied, explaining that during the man's trials and sufferings was when he had been *carried* by the Lord, and thus the one set of footprints visible in the sand. It is such a beautiful illustration of God's faithfulness to us in the darkest of days.

In my mind's eye, I can also imagine God using members of his body to do this heavy lifting. Squinting toward the wet sand, I see the size 9 shoe print of my pastor. I see the long-toed imprint of a lifetime friend. I see the tiny footprint of my precious grandson. In the midst of my own trials, time and time again, God has used these precious ones to carry me through the worst of the storm. When my own feet have failed, the imprint of their care has so melted into God's that I cannot distinguish between them.

## Passing the Peace

One ancient ritual I love, still practiced in many liturgical churches, is termed "the passing of the peace." The tradition is based on common greetings in Scripture. For example, Jesus would often greet his disciples with the words "Peace be with you." Paul opened his letters with the words "Grace and peace be with you." "Passing the peace" typically occurs sometime during a worship service, when parishioners turn to their neighbors, grasp their hands, look into their eyes, and speak the words "The peace of the Lord be with you" and receive the words in turn, "And also with you." To wish God's peace upon another brother or sister in Christ in greeting and recognition of grace is a beautiful concept, full of rich symbolism. But there must be substance behind the ritual, if it is to be full of meaning and truth in our actual lives in community.

In his letter to the Romans, Paul spoke of the body of Christ, its importance and its practical functions, and then drops in this piece of advice: "If it is possible, as far as it depends on you, live at peace with everyone" (Romans 12:18). What would it look like to, in essence, "pay forward" to everyone we meet the peace that Christ has given us?

We bring the peace of Christ when we band together for someone whose burden has become too overwhelming for one or two to carry. The Scriptures tell us to carry our own loads, the hassles of daily living we all have to handle. But we are also told to "carry each other's burdens" (Galatians 6:2). A burden is a super load, if you will. It is an enormous, insurmountable thud of pain or need that lands in someone's life. Gene and Carol Kent's beautiful and benevolent life of writing, serving, and ministry to others was suddenly challenged beyond their wildest dreams, when they got a phone call that sent them reeling: Their only son, Jason—a strong Christian leader all his life, a graduate of the Naval Academy, a newlywed and new stepfather—had been arrested for murder. Out of fear for the safety of his young stepdaughters, Jason shot and killed the girls' father, and was eventually sentenced to life in prison without parole.

During the long emotionally and physically crushing months between Jason's arrest and conviction, friends who loved Gene and Carol gathered to form a support circle of strength and love around their family. A few of them had reflected upon the New Testament story of how the friends of a paralytic carried the disabled man to Jesus on a stretcher, lowering him through a hole in a roof so that the Master could see and perhaps heal him. There are times in our lives when even the strongest men and women of faith are paralyzed with overwhelming sorrow and stress. We can't move. We can't think. We cannot even find the wherewithal to utter a prayer. We need others to help us carry the burden that is simply too heavy for one. Gene and Carol's circle of loving friends dubbed themselves "stretcher bearers," and provided service and help to the hurting couple in dozens of practical ways, along with prayer and encouragement. From coupons for takeout meals to visits to Jason in prison, to vouchers for flights and hotel rooms to gifts of time and support for Jason's grieving new bride and her children, tangible love poured forth every month during the worst of the crisis. Gene and Carol were devastated, but they were never alone.

It is amazing what can be borne, eventually and with God's help, if we know we are not alone in our pain and trauma.[2] Like soldiers in the stories of The Band of Brothers, we bond deeply and forever because we do not leave one of our wounded behind in battle. I think of the many ministries that rally around communities that suffer devastation from tornadoes, floods, or hurricanes. Teams of caring people on short- and long-term missions, who go to provide ongoing help in Third World countries, accomplishing together what they could never do alone. The Salvation Army and Red Cross are living, breathing "stretcher bearers" to thousands of over-burdened souls every day, bringing Christ's tangible peace to souls in turmoil.

## The Family God Provides

Sarah, thirty, lived with a cognitive disability. Always quick with a smile, Sarah was a delight to all who knew her. She had lived in a string of different group homes since she was eighteen years old. Both Sarah's parents had died during that time and her siblings had all moved out of state. Most days, Sarah felt very alone.

One day, when she was getting ready to go to work at a local day-care center, Sarah collapsed. Rushed to the hospital, she was diagnosed with a chronic heart condition. While her health could be managed with diet, exercise, and medication, the home in which she lived wasn't equipped or licensed to care for her. During the moment in her life when she most needed stability, Sarah was shipped off to live in yet another home.

At the new home, Sarah began attending church with Janet, the staff member who worked every Sunday morning. It was a small neighborhood Baptist church, and the folks who worshiped there quickly took a liking to Sarah. For the first time in a very long time, Sarah felt loved and valued. At church suppers, and other activities, members of the congregation would learn more about her family and her life, her hopes and her dream of being a preschool teacher. After attending the church for about a year, Sarah was baptized and was celebrated with a lavish reception.

One in a string of storms in Sarah's life became that place—that one-set-of-footprints place—where she was carried and buoyed and loved by the community of faith. The promise of God she was hearing about in church that he would never leave her or forsake her was being made real through the people of God. They had become, for Sarah, the knowable presence of God's love for her.

## Peacemaking Comes With Risks

While there are some beautiful redemptive stories, like Sarah's, when the body of Christ functions as it was meant to function, the "after" picture isn't always as perfect as we'd like it to be. Sometimes, when we pour ourselves out for another, we wonder if God has worked through us at all. I doubt there is a true peacemaker alive who has not, at times, felt used or tricked or hurt. There is at times a cost to being a person of generosity and peaceful service. Alas, the promise of Jesus is not "Blessed are the peacemakers because every time you attempt to bring peace you will be richly rewarded with responsive and grateful people." He only promised that God would see and acknowledge our childlike open hearts—that these acts of peacemaking would not go unnoticed by the Father.

Sure we want to be wise with our time and resources, but we cannot hedge all our bets. There are some risks involved in bringing Christ's peace to a messed-up world. The following piece was found written and hanging on a wall in Mother Teresa's home for children in Calcutta, India. The words have been widely attributed to her. Wise words from a woman awarded the world's highest award for bringing more peace on earth in 1979, The Nobel Peace Prize. If you've grown weary or jaded in well-doing, this will help bring a measure of peace to your heart.

> People are often unreasonable, irrational, and self-centered.
> Forgive them anyway.
>
> If you are kind, people may accuse you of selfish, ulterior motives.
> Be kind anyway.
>
> If you are successful, you will win some unfaithful friends and some genuine enemies.
> Succeed anyway.
>
> If you are honest and sincere, people may deceive you.
> Be honest and sincere anyway.
>
> What you spend years creating, others could destroy overnight.
> Create anyway.
>
> If you find serenity and happiness, some may be jealous.
> Be happy anyway.
>
> The good you do today will often be forgotten.
> Do good anyway.
>
> Give the best you have, and it will never be enough.
> Give your best anyway.
>
> In the final analysis, it is between you and God.
> It was never between you and them anyway.[3]

Perhaps this is why Jesus emphasized over and over again that when we give or serve or "pass the peace" of Christ to another human soul, we need to do it with the motive that we are showing gratitude to God for the mercy he's shown us. If we do it for any other motive—to change someone, to receive thanks or praise—we will only be stressed rather than filled with peace.

"Pass the peace" as unto the Lord and for no other reason, and your life will be a living vessel of calm and serenity in a world of uncertain storms.

> Let the peace of Christ rule in your hearts, since as members of one body you were called to peace. And be thankful.
>
> Colossians 3:15

# 9

# Peace From a Balanced Brain

> Fits of depression come over most of us. Usually cheerful as we may be, we must at intervals be cast down. The strong are not always vigorous, the wise not always ready, the brave not always courageous, and the joyous not always happy.[1]
>
> Charles Spurgeon

Anyone who has ever owned or loved or even sort of liked a dog—or knows someone else who does—can't help but be drawn into John Grogan's book *Marley & Me*. Within a few pages, millions of readers have found themselves swallowing a lump in their throat while simultaneously laughing aloud at this lovable lug of a pet.

I sense that readers smiled about this beloved disaster of a dog with a heart of gold and a keen knack for destruction because, in part, we also recognize something of ourselves in Marley, especially in our most vulnerable, frightened, confused, and embarrassing moments.

Though Marley was a loyal and loving Labrador most of the time, when the raindrops began, and the thunder boomed, and darkness fell, and storms rolled in, Marley went out of his ever-lovin' canine mind. His owners would try to rush home to give him a tranquilizer, prescribed by the vet, at the first sight and sound of thunder and lightning, because they'd seen the damage Marley could do when he went AWOL, trying to dig his way out of the house and away from whatever unseen terror triggered him.

John's wife, Jenny, hurried home during one particular rainstorm and what she saw left her almost speechless with disbelief. From the book it says it was as if she "had just walked in and discovered a body hanging from the chandelier." She found the dog "panting frantically, paws and mouth bleeding. Loose fur was everywhere, as though the thunder had scared the hair right out of his coat." The damage was unfathomable. "An entire wall was gouged open, obliterated clear down to the studs. Plaster and wood chips and bent nails were everywhere. Electric wiring lay exposed. Blood smeared the floor and the walls. It looked, literally, like the scene of a shotgun homicide."[2]

Though John never liked sedating Marley, the pills helped his furry buddy "move past the deadly threat that existed only in his mind." Grogan wrote, "If he were human, I would call him certifiably psychotic. He was delusional, paranoid, convinced a dark, evil force was coming from the heavens to take him. I knelt beside him and stroked his blood-caked fur. 'Geez, dog,' I said, 'What are we going to do with you?' Without lifting his head, he looked up at me with those bloodshot stoner eyes of his, the saddest, most mournful eyes I have ever seen, and just gazed at me. It was as if he were trying to tell me something, something important he needed me to understand. 'I know,' I said, 'I know you can't help it.'"[3]

Who among humanity has not had a Marley moment or two? When you've been so frightened or depressed or triggered that you temporarily took leave of your senses? And perhaps when you finally calmed down and surveyed the damage around you, wondered, "What in the heck just happened?" If you are blessed, you've had a John Grogan-ish friend who met you on the floor of your life, looked into your eyes, and understood that this is not the real you. This is a broken, as-yet-unhealed aspect of you, triggered by fear and dark thoughts or old traumas. Or a quirky brain.

## A Brain Out of Balance

In my book *Relentless Pursuit,* I describe my struggles with and the shame surrounding adult attention deficit disorder (ADD). "On a bad day," I wrote, "the ADD brain is like having a roomful of preschoolers in your head, all out of their seats, climbing over desks, poking at each other, some whining at the window to go outside, others racing up and down the aisles, still others throwing erasers across the room at the ones by the window, while the teacher stands behind her desk, shouting at them to sit down and turn to page ten in their books." ADD often comes with the territory of creative, all-over-the-map personalities. "On a good day, with help, the children in my brain can be compelled to sit still," and "they come up with new ways of seeing and original means of self-expression."

Perhaps you saw the movie *Up,* and the hilarious and easily distracted talking dog named Doug, who loses all focus at any sighting of a squirrel. The gag repeats itself throughout the movie, with Doug trying to remain engaged, but then is instantly distracted, often mid-sentence, by thoughts of a squirrel. In fact, the Urban Dictionary now has a definition for the term *squirrel*! "A SQUIRREL!!! moment is when you have been distracted by random nothingness. To be diverted from one task/situation with no effort. To have one's attention easily diverted."

Having ADD is a bit of a Catch-22, because I need a certain amount of stimulation with input from a variety of sources in order to write. But then when I begin to try to organize the piles of notes I've gathered from thoughts, books, films, quotes, the Internet, music (onto legal pads, napkins, and Post-it notes) into some sort of cohesive order, I look at the scattered piles and get completely overwhelmed. At this point my brain simply shuts down and leaves the building, calling over its shoulder, "To heck with this!"

Alas, even though I sometimes feel out of step with humanity, it appears I can relate very well to at least two dogs: one real and anxious, and one cartoon dog driven to distraction. Because mingled with my attention-challenged brain that is at the same time everywhere and nowhere, is also a brain that is prone to an anxious depression. Sometimes it is just a mild melancholy of the artsy-angsty sort, but in other seasons it is of the chronically "heavy black lead coat" variety known as chemical depression. In these times, I look out at the world, at God, and at people, and when my brain is unbalanced, I see nothing but an expanse of hopelessness, shame, and darkness.

Now throw into the mix most of the characteristics listed in the book *The Highly Sensitive Person* and *Seasons of Discontent and Distraction* and you've got a lulu of a Marley/Doug hybrid situation. I honestly do not know how some of my friends, family members, and professional colleagues cope with me in these times of scattered despair, when I am ineffective and wandering off-line in search of a dark cloud under which I can ponder the meaningless of my existence.

In truth, some people could not bear up under my quirks and moods, starts and stops, foggy and poor or impulsive decisions. They had to walk away to save their sanity. I did not blame them; or if I did at the time, I do not any longer. Even I get fed up with the challenge of living with myself when my brain is malfunctioning.

But there's something redemptive and hopeful about the sentence I just wrote above. Because of a compassionate Christian therapist who understands and explained to me how the human brain works, I now realize that there is "Ken," the soul who is always and forever a beloved child of God, whose heart longs to follow and serve him and others; then there is "Ken's Brain," that gives me a boatload of trouble when it is not in balance and full of the right nutrients, oxygen, and neurotransmitters. I am not my brain, though I am responsible to care for my brain now that I know what to do. When my brain works right, I am a much happier, more productive and fun person to be with and live with. Problems no longer seem insurmountable, creative thought returns, peace surrounds. God seems oh so much nicer. I remember that he is on my side, cheering me on rather than wringing his hands in disbelief and discouragement at the huge disappointment I feel I must be.

I have noticed that Christians, especially, are prone to mistake their off-kilter brains for the idea that we are permanently character-flawed, unworthy, or sinful—that we ourselves are one giant mistake. One of the most peace-giving revelations and

Aha! moments for me came when I got a real look at the inside working of my own hurting and complicated brain.

It all began with an out-of-the-blue phone call from an old friend, Greg Johnson, who would soon become John Grogan to my Inner Marley. "Ken, I know you've had your share of struggles with depression and distraction. My wife Becky has ADD too. Like you, she is especially sensitive in ways that makes her an intuitive writer and tenderhearted friend, but over-sensitivity sometimes leaves her feeling raw and exposed. She was also recently diagnosed with post-traumatic stress disorder (PTSD), so she understands a lot of what you may be dealing with. She just finished writing a book with a Christian therapist, Dr. Earl Henslin, a colleague of the brain expert Dr. Daniel Amen, about the role the brain plays in everything from our moods, focus, and even connection to God. She had her brain scanned as part of the research for the book, and it was a life-altering experience. I think this book and coming over for supper and chatting with Becky might encourage you. Give you some fresh hope. You've got so much heart and talent, buddy. I just think you might have a brain that needs the right help."

He shared a copy of *This Is Your Brain on Joy,* and by the time I closed the book, I was daring to hope that perhaps I wasn't a wash-up after all, that there could be practical help and hope I hadn't yet tried. I followed this up with more discussions with Greg and Becky at their home over a home-cooked meal, a few tears, some healing laughter, and reminiscing.

Though many people are helped by the information in the book alone, or a phone counseling session with Dr. Henslin, in my case, which was more complicated, we all thought it would be especially helpful to get a brain scan, along with a face-to-face diagnosis and consultation. It cost more than I could afford, but anonymous donors (God bless you, whoever you are) pitched in, and the next thing I knew I had my head in a SPECT scan machine as it ticked and clicked and took pictures of my noggin.

I can't describe the relief to discover that, first of all, there was, indeed, a brain in my skull. But, not surprisingly, the scans revealed I had a brain in need of rescue. This was actually a relief to me because with the diagnosis came a clear plan of action. When you've given up hope, nothing sounds more beautiful than the words from a compassionate professional saying, "I see your problems, here and here. Don't worry, it is fixable. We can help you." I was given a protocol to follow that included a couple of pinpointed medications and brain-healthy supplements, along with encouragement to exercise daily, eat nutrient-dense food, and get regular restorative sleep.

Not terribly spiritual-sounding, is it? And yet this one day with a therapist who understands the brain, gave me the first grip on hope that I'd felt in ages. I fell asleep in peace, awoke in gratitude, ready to begin the process of getting my brain back into balance.

It did not happen overnight, but with time and a few tweaks, the heavy black coat of depression began to lighten into a sort of grayish sweater, and then one day I felt something I recognized like a long lost friend: a hint of happiness. During this time, friends new and old encouraged me. Greg met me at the gym for walks on the treadmill. "You need oxygen to your brain, Ken!" he'd encourage. Clarity came to me as I began writing again. Creativity blossomed. I took a few speaking engagements and felt the old joy of being a vessel of God's encouragement to others again. I even saw that my own struggles, failures, limitations, and weaknesses could be redeemed and used to help others who, like me, despaired of ever feeling normal, much less beloved, wanted, and needed. After a few more months on a brain-healing program, my eldest daughter said, "Dad, the old you is finally back!" I didn't realize it, but she told me it had been about seven years since she'd felt that I was my best and truest self.

I would like to end this chapter by telling you, "And then my brain and I lived happily ever after." But the truth is that I have had times when I've stopped taking good care of my brain, and inevitably I'm a ball of messy, confused, depressed emotions again. The difference is that now I know what to do to get balanced again. Taking care of your brain is part of taking care of this temple we've been entrusted with. Some days I do a better job than others, and even the best brains can get the blues sometimes. I've learned, for example, that because our brains are deprived of food during the night, many of us wake up with a sense of impending doom, feeling as if God himself is frowning at us. I learned that brains need healthy Omega-3 fatty acids the way car gears need grease to operate smoothly. I learned that just walking for thirty minutes a day is a mood lifter and prevents cognitive decline, even Alzheimer's disease. I'm still learning.

## Jesus Cares About Your Brain Health

One of the stories I have come to love is the one told in Mark 6 about Jesus feeding the five thousand. In it we can see clearly how concerned our Savior is about feeding us, nourishing us, brain and soul. He sees the body and soul intertwined, and has particular compassion on his creatures when we are tired or hungry.

In this unfolding story, the apostles had been out on a long mission, and they were gathering together again, overflowing with news they wanted to share, to tell Jesus "all that they had done and taught." Their Teacher was surely pleased, but he also noticed something they might have been too busy and excited to detect: They were exhausted. At one point, Jesus said, "Come off by yourselves; let's take a break and get a little rest" (vv. 30–31 The Message). Mark notes that there was "constant coming and going; they didn't even have time to eat."

Have you ever been so caught up in busyness that you forgot to eat or pause to rest? Until your brain and body start to feel the effects of low-blood sugar: a headache comes on, sometimes the shakes, the crankiness and inability to put two coherent thoughts together. Like the V-8 commercial, we figuratively slap our hand against our forehead and think, *I should have stopped to rest and eat!*

Jesus is practicing preventative care as he ponders the experiences the disciples have just been through and foresees the journey ahead. He wants his friends to be at their best, and so he encourages them to be kind to their minds and bodies by getting on a boat and sailing away to a peaceful place for nourishment and a nap.

It turned out to be a brilliant idea. Because as Jesus and the disciples headed off for a little R & R, someone spotted them, and the word soon spread of the "rock star" in town. By the time Jesus and the boat of men pulled back up to shore, there was a crowd of five thousand plus people looking lost and confused, eyes fixed on Jesus in hope and expectation. Storms are not always a result of bad things happening: Sometimes storms arrive in the form of wonderful and positive things. They just happen to be overwhelming in scope.

Jesus being who he is, Mark's gospel says, "At the sight of them, his heart broke—like sheep with no shepherd they were. He went right to work teaching them" (v. 34 THE MESSAGE). Because Jesus had insisted that the disciples take time to replenish their brains with rest and food, they too were ready to roll and serve and give again. They could be fresh and help Jesus to handle this huge crowd with inner peace and calm.

At least to a point.

As the sun began to drop in the sky, the apostles' bellies began to growl with hunger, and their now tired brains were begging for a break. At this juncture, the disciples encouraged Jesus to say a little closing prayer so everyone could call it a day and go get some grub.

Then came the shocker: "You do it. Fix supper for them" (v. 37 THE MESSAGE), Jesus said.

The disciples thought he was joking. As if they were wealthy enough to buy food for this hillside full of people? *Very funny, Jesus.*

As the story goes, Jesus was serious and asked them to bring him whatever food they could find. All they could scrounge up was a small boy's picnic lunch: five small bread rolls and two fish. Scholars believe the fish were most likely sardines, of great abundance in the Sea of Galilee.

Interesting thing about sardines: They are extremely high in Omega-3's—richer in this brain-nourishing ingredient than even salmon. Bread in those days was made from unprocessed wheat and grains. So the lunch may have been small, but it packed a powerful neuron-restoring punch.

You know the rest of the story. Jesus lifted his face up to heaven, blessed the bread, and gave it to the disciples to distribute. He did the same with the two tiny sardines. And to everyone's amazement, the food multiplied; everyone ate until they were full and happy, their minds sharper and more focused. There were twelve baskets of food left over, like twelve doggie bags, one for each wide-eyed, awestruck disciple to carry home to the boat with them.

These are times when it must have been awfully fun to be Jesus.

After the meal was finished, Jesus, again looking out for the mental and physical stamina of his friends, insisted they go on ahead to the boat while he took care of finishing up with the crowd. Then Jesus took care of himself and his needs, climbing up a mountain to be alone and pray for a while. After all, it had been a hard day of serving and giving, even for the Son of God.

After I speak and encourage a crowd of people, I feel as though I've given every ounce of energy I have to give. I wish I had the stamina to meet with every person who was touched by something I said, precious people who want to visit and talk some more, one on one. I know there are many who need and desire an hour of counseling or a few minutes of compassion. And yet my human limitations start to take over after giving all I have to give. I am exhausted, usually famished, in search of restorative sleep and silence. I pray that the Lord will send the right people to help minister to those I cannot possibly meet with because I am physically unable to do so.

It comforts me to see that Jesus knows this about me, the way he knew this about his disciples and the five thousand on the hillside. He knew they needed food and rest and solitude before and after times of intense ministry or simply giving of themselves.

God, who created us, knows we function at our best when we receive the restorative powers of rest, food, water, sunshine, human love and belonging, time to walk and get exercise in fresh air, a healthy rhythm of solitude and community, and sessions of prayerful meditation. And when all these things are not enough to keep our brains functioning well, some of us are enormously grateful for supplements, medicine, and brilliant doctors who understand brain function.

When life gets tough and intense, or disorienting, when you are in a life transition, when the circumstantial storms start to thunder and swell, this is the time to make sure you practice good brain and soul care as often as you can; it is a very practical part of finding his peace in turmoil.

## Our Brains, Our Bodies, His Temple

A few months after I began feeling my old self again, I took Greg and Becky to dinner with earnings from a project I'd been able to write, thanks to renewed focus and returning joy. The restaurant is housed in an old stone church and so is creatively named The Old Stone Church. The lights were low, and the glowing candles cast beautiful colors on the stained-glass windows around us. The food was gourmet, the waiters attentive. We leisurely talked of the long broken roads that we've traversed, separately and together, over our many years of friendship. We spoke of movies and music and books and friends that have spoken to us in hours of need. Becky reminded me of words I'd said to her years ago in a moment of deep sorrow, confusion, and transition. Greg shared how my words have often inspired him to a greater love for Jesus. And I tell my two friends, with tears in my eyes, how grateful I am for their friendship and help in this last long and difficult season, when I could not see a future or a hope.

The waiter pours a good Pinot Noir, and we lift our glasses around the table in this sanctuary-turned-restaurant and make a toast. It is a peaceful, holy moment. I realize we are in a place that was once a chapel of worship where spiritual needs were met, and is now a place where good food and wine and kind attention are served as physical needs are tended to.

And I cannot help but wonder if both are, in essence, the same thing.

> Or didn't you realize that your body is a sacred place, the place of the Holy Spirit? Don't you see that you can't live however you please, squandering what God paid such a high price for? The physical part of you is not some piece of property belonging to the spiritual part of you. God owns the whole works. So let people see God in and through your body.
>
> 1 Corinthians 6:19 The Message

# 10

# Peace From Insightful Books and Movies

No form of art goes beyond ordinary consciousness as film does, straight to our emotions, deep into the twilight room of the soul.[1]

Ingmar Bergman

Whenever you read a good book, somewhere in the world a door opens to allow in more light.[2]

Vera Nazarian

The 1980 film *The Elephant Man*, featuring Anthony Hopkins and Anne Bancroft, is based on the true story of John Merrick, a man living in nineteenth-century London, whose face was severely deformed. The movie traces Merrick's rescue from sideshow degradation to being recognized as a person of dignity.

Those who came to know him recognized Merrick's great love for the arts, and musical theater in particular. Because being in public had been so very traumatic, he had never once in his lifetime attended. As the film concludes, when the end of his life is near, he has the opportunity to go to the theater. Looking very dapper in tux and white tie, Merrick is seated with his friends in the Royal Box seat with Princess Alexandra.

As the performance concludes, his friend Mrs. Kendal takes the stage to announce to the audience that the entire cast has chosen to dedicate the performance to Mr. John Merrick. Glancing up toward the Royal Box, she is beaming. As the audience begins to clap, they also glance up to see John Merrick. As the applause increases, all in the theater rise to offer him a standing ovation. His friends gently touch his elbow, encouraging him to stand in acknowledgment. It is a beautiful moment.

That evening, back at the hospital, Merrick expresses his gratitude to his surgeon. When Dr. Treves leaves, Merrick carefully completes a model he'd been constructing of a nearby church as the moving notes of Samuel Barber's *Adagio for Strings* play in the background. Reflecting a sketch hanging on the wall of a peaceful sleeping child, Merrick removes the pillows from his bed, which have kept him in an upright position, and lies down and dies.

The memory of Merrick's final preparations is one that has meant so much to me as I've searched for meaning in the storm. What ostensibly appears to be marked by absence, death itself, is full of rich presence and significance. I've found comfort in the memory of this moving scene.

## Power of Story

Throughout history, God has comforted his people with stories that brought meaning and understanding to their lives. Before anyone had ever laid hands on a personal leather-bound pocket Bible, these stories were passed down, orally, generation after generation. Parents told their children of the mighty acts of God, and those children told their children. By hearing how God had worked in the lives of others, people were given vision to recognize God at work in their own.

In the earliest days, God's people told stories of creation, God forming a man from the mud of the ground. They learned how God engaged with human beings in the stories of Abraham, Isaac, Jacob, and Joseph. New generations would discover afresh the character of God as they listened to these stories passed down by their ancestors. They came to know what a good king was like in the stories of David. They understood the meaning of suffering in the stories of exile and punishment.

Israel's most important story, over the centuries, was the story of God's gracious deliverance out of Egypt. Enslaved by the Egyptians, suffering under their cruel taskmasters, the Hebrew people cried out to God. Hearing their cry, God sent them a deliverer in the person of Moses. Parting the sea by God's power, with mighty upstretched arms, Moses delivered the people from oppression. When Pharaoh's soldiers pursued them, the roaring waters crashed down upon them, crushing them.

Gathered around the fire on cool evenings, families would have heard this amazing story and in it found meaning for their own lives. Hearing of a God who noticed the hurt of his people and turned an ear toward their cries, they would have begun to recognize God's posture toward them. Discovering that despite the fierce powers that would seek to thwart redemption, they'd know in the deepest places of their hearts that God was relentless in his commitment to his people. Learning that God worked miracles in the most hopeless situations, they would have gleaned comfort and strength for their own lives. In the stories of God's faithfulness to those who had come before, a holy imagination was birthed in the hearts and minds of those who heard them. In the stories of God's power to protect his people from the mighty walls of water that threatened to overwhelm, God's people discovered the One who would protect *them* from waters that threatened to overwhelm.

## My Comfort

As a boy, my father brought me great comfort when I was afraid. On many nights I'd be tucked into my bed, and something would get into my mind that I couldn't quite shake loose. I might have been spooked by a willowy shadow dancing across the wall or by the memory of a scary book I'd just read. I would call out for my dad, and he would sit on the edge of my bed and, with his strong presence, calm my fears.

When I read *To Kill a Mockingbird*, I am reminded, in the steadfast presence of Atticus Finch, of my father's calm and comforting presence. At the end of the book, when Scout comes home at night, she finds her father sitting at the side of her brother Jem's bed. Curling up next to her father, she listens to him read one of Jem's books aloud. No sooner does Scout fall asleep than she feels Atticus' boot gently nudging her ribs. Rousing his groggy daughter while she denies slumber by protesting that she's heard every word of the story, he leads her to her room and helps her into her pajamas.

Author Harper Lee describes Atticus's gentle exit from Scout's room, "He turned out the light and went into Jem's room. He would be there all night, and he would be there when Jem awoke the morning."[3]

Those final two lines of the classic American novel bring me such comfort. For one child, Atticus read and guided and dressed, finally tucking sleepy Scout in under her covers. For his other child, Atticus's sturdy presence through the night was a silent witness to his presence and steadfast comfort. The way in which this scene evokes such warm memories of my own father comforts me in my deep places.

## The Story That Is True

No one understood the power of a story well-told more than British writer C. S. Lewis. A contemporary of J. R. R. Tolkien, Lewis was a proud intellectual atheist before humbly turning over his life to Christ. One evening in a British pub, during the 1930s, Lewis and Tolkien talked long into the night about faith and literature. Already soft to the possibility that truth could be known through mythological stories, Lewis remained unconvinced that any of the myths of a dying and rising god, so firmly believed in various forms by cultures around the globe, stood out among the others. That evening, however, Tolkien argued that in the person of Jesus Christ, the story *really happened.* That conversation, between academics who loved to argue and persuade, turned out to be the one that changed Lewis's heart. He returned home that evening and prayed for the first time to a God whom he was willing to know.

Lewis's fantasy series for children, *The Chronicles of Narnia*, would be added to the canon of literature that included a dying and rising redeemer. In the world of Narnia, Lewis's White Witch had cast a curse, subjecting all the land to the Hundred-Years Winter. The mighty lion Aslan, in his death and resurrection, liberates the world of Narnia from the reign of the terrible, icy queen. In this work of creative fiction, and so many others, Lewis tells a story that is true, one that would echo with veracity for generations in readers' deep places. In his words, those suffering their own Hundred-Years Winter would be warmed to the One who redeems.

God uses books like Lewis's, as well as film, poetry, and plays that tell stories that are deeply true. Just as Lewis himself was guided toward Truth through stories that reflected the One that is true, so we too have access to the One who calms storms. Through the creative stories others have told, we can find real hope and peace in God's mercies.

## A Transforming Read

When from the outside his life looked the brightest—a job he enjoyed, married a few years, having just welcomed a new baby son—Kevin was hurting. The arrival of his son had triggered old feelings of sadness about the father he'd never known. It became more and more difficult to get out of bed each morning. Food had lost its taste. On the weekends, Kevin could only fall back into bed after breakfast. Though most of his family and friends didn't realize the severity of his pain, his wife was concerned. She suspected Kevin was suffering with depression, but she had no idea how to help.

One Saturday afternoon, unable to sleep and unable to hoist himself to life, Kevin glanced over at a small pile of books beside the baby's bassinet that his wife had been reading. While *What to Expect the First Year* was dog-eared and bent and bookmarked, a slimmer volume appeared untouched and caught Kevin's eye. The desolate winter scene on the cover seemed a perfect picture of his present reality. Recalling there had been a group at his church that had studied *The Shack*, he opened the cover and read a page or two.

The wicked ice storm detailed in the opening pages seemed an apt picture of his current emotional paralysis. Though he suspected that reading about someone else's painful life, when his own felt so unmanageable, might not be the best idea, he kept reading. How had this uneventful story of one man's sadness, he wondered, garnered so much attention among so many? Within a chapter or two, he understood why.

When William P. Young's protagonist, Mack, encounters the person of God in the bodies of three very unique *physical* persons, a dim light began to shine into Kevin's darkness. In these unlikely manifestations of the Holy One, Kevin's weary eyes opened to a new possibility. What if, Kevin began to wonder, God was not a father who abandoned his children, not one who left, or even who died? What if he was a gracious Father who saw his pain and longed to embrace him? Though it wasn't a quick magic fix, a tiny flicker of hope had been ignited in Kevin's heart. What if God was *other* than he had ever imagined? In the pages of another's pain, Kevin found a warm island of peace in the frozen chill his life had become.

God's fierce pursuit of Kevin's heart could not be thwarted by the emotional freeze Kevin was enduring. It could not be stopped because Kevin was for a period of time unable to pray. It wouldn't be derailed because the words of Scripture had begun to ring hollow in Kevin's ears. It wouldn't be hindered because Kevin wasn't able to reach out for help to his community of faith. Rather, with all the creativity of the One who created in the beginning, God had warmed Kevin's cool heart, granting shelter in the storm through the pages of a book he almost didn't pick up.

## Peace Through Beauty

The sensory-engaging power of certain *movies* is also able to touch a very special place within us. The 1992 film *A River Runs Through It* tells the story of the two sons of a Presbyterian minister, Reverend Maclean. The movie is set in Missoula, Montana, in the 1920s. One of the pastor's sons is the stereotypical rebellious "pastor's kid," while the other is more solidly grounded in the faith. All that connects them, through no tenuous thread, is their love for fly-fishing. The sheer beauty of the footage shot on several of Montana's majestic rivers brings me calm and peace as I watch water cascade over canyon rocks. Even on a screen, it is breathtaking!

Have you encountered God's magnificent presence in films or books that were able to capture something of God's power? It may be a riveting *Animal Planet* documentary on the wilderness pecking order of species. It may be a book that describes in vivid detail the wonder of the galaxies. Or it may be a poem that so aptly paints a single rose petal that you are moved to lift your eyes to the heavens. Books and movies, poetry and prose, bearing witness to God's mighty works, can point us toward the One who creates and redeems when life is hard.

## Comfort in Loss

When I am being tossed about on an ocean of chaos, what I most want is to know that I am not alone. Depending on the nature of the storm, it may be that I actually *am* in the boat by myself. In these dark moments, I've received the gift of presence in the pages of various books. In them I'm given confidence that when things look the darkest, I am ultimately *not* alone.

When hemmed in by darkness, as I squint my eyes to read by candlelight, I do not turn to stories of light and life. These narratives are so far from my experience, they leave me feeling thirstier and hungrier than when I began. However, I have found great solace in the stories of those who have been honest about loss and grief. When authors tell a story that is true about life and suffering, I am no longer alone.

In my journey, one of these life-giving books has been *A Grief Observed*. In the wake of his wife's death from cancer, author C. S. Lewis reflects on the meaning of life and faith in this authentic memoir. Honest about his doubts, Lewis expresses the deep agony of heart, which I have also known. In a similar genre, one that does not avoid the reality of pain endured, I have turned to *Lament for a Son* by Nicholas Wolterstorff. When Wolsterstorff lost his twenty-five-year-old son in a mountain-climbing accident, he began a journey to give voice to his loss and grief. Neither volume offers easy answers, but each serves as a companion to those of us who suffer grief, assuring us that we are not alone in our suffering.

## Encounters of Redemption

Though I find it hard to fathom, Paul, a friend of mine, has watched the 2009 *Star Trek* movie *thirteen* times! The first five or six times he paid ten dollars to watch the surround-sound version in theaters. Subsequently, since the release of the DVD version, he's watched it at home on the small screen. There is, for my friend, something deeply true and compelling about the story depicted by film producers.

In the opening scene, the futuristic ship soaring through space encounters a threat from outside that quickly rises to crisis level. When the ship's captain is required to shuttle over to the attacking vessel, he places Lieutenant Kirk in charge of the ship. In a dramatically woven plot, as his young wife labors to deliver their firstborn, Kirk orders the immediate evacuation of the vessel, which faces imminent destruction. His intention is to put the ship on autopilot and to join her, but at the last minute, the autopilot fails. If the lives of many are to be saved, Kirk must remain at the helm.

On the future's version of cell phones, Kirk continues to converse with and comfort his wife. She delivers a son, and in the midst of the chaos they choose together to name the child Jim. As Lieutenant Kirk continues to assure his bride that he'll soon join her in safety, he knows he will never leave the doomed ship. And he doesn't.

The collision of birth and death, lives saved and lives lost, is a poignant one. In fact, it has moved my friend Paul to tears no less than thirteen times. In the fictional scene, Paul is reminded of the deeply true story of the life of one man that was given, in love, to save many.

The best way to understand what a movie has to say to us

is to reflect on the moments like these that move us, for they open a window to the soul. Through that window, we can look momentarily into the depths of who we are. What we see could be something in our past, our future, or even something in the present. We may see our hunger and thirst for the first time. We may see our deepest fears, cowering for expression, or the wings of our most beautiful dreams. We may see the open sore that is our woundedness. Or the beginnings of its healing. We may see our shame—or deliverance from that shame. We may see our sin. Or our salvation.

We may see heaven calling to us. We may even see Jesus—or his shadow as he passes by. In those moments we are most vulnerable to grace. For through them God reaches out to us—sometimes to instruct or correct, sometimes to move us forward or turn us around, sometimes to lift us to our feet or to bring us to our knees. But at all times to draw us to himself.

## Stories That Are Deeply True

Perhaps you have been equally moved by a story that points you to themes of redemption. Or perhaps you've read a compelling memoir. Although its storyline bears no resemblance to your own, you experienced, nonetheless, being deeply seen and heard and known in its pages. Or perhaps you've watched a movie and been convinced that, although it was ostensibly not a story from a *Christian* viewpoint, it told a deeply true story, which brought meaning to your own. Or maybe you have read a poem that for reasons you weren't able to fully understand, gave you a sense of unexpected peace during a difficult season. During those perilous times when we are *least* able to receive God's grace in the most traditional ways, when we are desperate for peace in the chaos of our lives, God's Spirit can minister through words that calm our hearts and bring meaning to our suffering. In the pages of a good book, in riveting scenes on a screen, in ancient dramas embodied by stage actors, God can meet you and touch your heart with his peace.

> When you come, bring the cloak that I left with Carpus at Troas, and my scrolls, especially the parchments.
>
> 2 Timothy 4:13

# 11

# Peace Through Serving Others

Lord, make me an instrument of Thy peace.[1]

Saint Francis of Assisi

While Jack was without a car for a season, he used the city bus to accomplish many of his daily errands. One day, returning home from the grocery store, he lumbered up the steps of the bus carrying a few bags of groceries and a box of fried chicken. Dropping into the closest available seat, he set the bags down beside him.

Across the aisle, Jack noticed an old man slumped against the window. His hair and beard were unkempt, his skin was weathered from the elements, and his clothes were rumpled and stained. A faint odor emanated throughout the front of the bus. By all appearances, the man was not only without a car, he was most likely without a home. Who knows, Jack figured, he may not have any friends either. Or know where his next meal is coming from.

Purposeful not to gawk, Jack continued to notice him from the corner of his eye throughout the ride. When the bus was within a block of Jack's stop, he began to gather his bags. As the driver came to a halt, Jack stood with his packages to make his way off the bus. Passing the man, Jack quietly slipped him his box of chicken.

Jack had been looking forward to a delicious fried chicken dinner that night. And yet, he reported, as he walked toward his home, he noticed that he suddenly didn't feel hungry anymore. He also noticed that he didn't feel whiny that he didn't have his own transportation. As Jack shared this with me, the exhortation of Mark Twain resonated in my heart: "The best way to cheer yourself up is to try to cheer somebody else up." What once sounded difficult at best, trite at worst, was proved deeply true in Jack's experience with a man whose name he did not know. He said that he felt more freedom and joy and peace from opening his hands to the stranger on the bus than he ever would have known had he remained stuck in his own experience.

I have also found this to be true, on many occasions, in my own experience. In the midst of my own storms, I do try to get out of myself as much as I can for this very reason. When I'm focused on myself and my problems, everything else gets out of focus. When my eyes are on my troubles, other people's needs begin to blur. Their heartaches seem less relevant. Their storms appear distant. In these moments, I find real relief as I purpose to look at other people and not to avert my gaze. I experience peace as I listen to them and do not tune them out.

## The Hard but Good Way

This isn't to say it's easy. Being aware of the world around you can be difficult when you are caught up in your own storm, when your heart is sinking, or when your losses are mounting. It's hard to be aware of the work God is doing both in you and around you. But coming to the end of ourselves can be a blessing in disguise. Sometimes throwing things overboard can actually be a good thing. Sometimes our ship running aground can be fortuitous, even providential, as it was when Paul's ship was wrecked, landing him on the island of Malta.

Malta was the place where God wanted to manifest his power and his goodness to people who didn't know him. So although Paul was headed to Rome, God's intentions toward others were realized in the wake of Paul's storm. One of those gracious intentions was God's heart toward the people of Malta. Malta, however, hadn't been on the captain's itinerary. It took a storm and a shipwreck to get Paul there. Just like it took persecution (Acts 8:1) to fulfill the promise Jesus made to the disciples (Acts 1:8).

We do not navigate toward stormy seas. When it is in our power, we avoid storm clouds. We never choose the terror of a shipwreck. We avoid it at all costs. We do not pray to endure loss. Our prayers beg for just the opposite. In the unfolding drama of God's salvation, however, these situations *we would not choose* can be the providential means to God's eternal ends.

## Surprising Efficacy

As we're being pelted during our own storms at sea, tossing a rescue line to another who is also struggling to stay afloat can have surprising results. While it seems almost counterintuitive, service to another can *buoy both*! In extending relief to someone else, we can experience peace in the midst of our own chaos.

This gift of God—to experience God's gentle grace in the service of others—is woven into the very fabric of our being. Time and time again, I've found that when I serve others, it puts my struggles in the background, putting them into perspective. When we stretch out an arm to serve others who are being tossed about by life's waves, we are girded with strength to endure our own. God's beautiful design is expressed in the wisdom of a wise proverb: "Help thy brother's boat across, and Lo! thine own has reached the shore."

## Reaching the Shore

Sam, a friend of mine, has pushed himself to compete in a number of triathlons over the years. He loves swimming. He tolerates running. He hates cycling. So when he was invited to celebrate the fiftieth birthday of a colleague with a fifty-mile bike ride, he balked. Then persuading himself that he'd enjoy the company, he joined about twelve other men for the grueling ride.

Of course, not all of them found it as grueling as Sam did. Some of them had fancy racing bikes, which Sam did not have. In fact, his rickety old bike wasn't really fit to leave the garage. Some of them had sleek biking clothing, which Sam did not. Though he'd often thought biker's shorts were a little much, the chafing that began at mile twelve changed his mind. Some of the other cyclists had been training in preparation, which Sam had not. In fact, he made a special point of not even touching his bike between races. Suffice to say, the event was less than a joyful celebration for Sam.

By the final quarter of the journey, Sam was really suffering. When he started to lag behind, however, someone would always hang back to chat, keeping Sam's mind off his pain. Struggling to ascend a half-mile rise, Burt sidled up to him. Placing his hand on the small of Sam's back, Burt—competent cyclist and consummate friend—helped push Sam and his ramshackle cycle all the way up the daunting hill. Though Burt didn't seem to be suffering as he was, Sam knew it could not have been an easy assist.

Struggling against the same gravity and friction that slowed Sam, by helping his weak brother's "boat" across, Burt found himself on the other side as well!

## Calm in My Storms

In my professional life, I've found this hand-on-the-back-of-another to be exactly what gets me up the steep mountain or across the raging sea. I try to respond to all my mail, email, Facebook comments, telephone calls. These are small things, but I want people to feel their worth, and that they matter. I often send books to those who've read one of my books and are moved to write me. Many are in the midst of personal storms so severe they feel they can't make it, so along with a book, I'll send a note of encouragement. Sometimes I write these notes when I'm feeling on top of the world and generous and full of faith. Sometimes I write them when I am struggling to keep my own chin up, trying to remember and believe that God loves me.

It may be that I'm behind in my work, caught up in a gale of emotions. At times I experience crippling waves of stress, fear of failure, fear of disappointing a client, shame, and much more. Often, during such times, a colleague or new writer will email me, needing some advice on their own work. Though initially the need can feel like a burden I'm not prepared to shoulder, I've slowly learned that these requests can function as God's grace to me! The little breaks I take from my own projects in order to respond—to trim the sail on someone else's project that is taking on water—have a calming effect on me. Perhaps it's the need to take a break from the fury of my own storm. Perhaps it's using other mental muscles and giving my own strained muscles a break. Whatever the reason, I've learned the lesson. And I've received these opportunities as God's calming presence in my storms.

These little breaks buoy me, as do the more intensive engagements.

During one of the worst seasons of my life, before I found good help to balance my brain, I found myself falling down a rabbit hole of clinical depression, and self-defeating thoughts plagued me daily. I was sure that my writing life was over and, in fact, I wondered if my life would ever take on any real meaning for God again. Unable to get my brain out of a dense fog and to focus, I failed my family, my friends, and watched helplessly as deadlines for projects came and went, unable to form a coherent thought. During this time, I met some precious fellow strugglers, and it was a comfort in many ways to be with others where there were no expectations for me to be "spiritual," but simply to be anonymous.

I met a woman and her middle-school-age daughter who were staying at the shelter one day. The daughter expressed a desire to be a writer, and even as I was fighting my own feelings of worthlessness, I found myself spending a few sessions with this young lady and her mom, explaining how I learned to write. My own pain lifted during the minutes I focused on encouraging someone else. Sometimes I think God uses us best, encourages us most, when we think we have nothing to offer. This experience changed me forever; I no longer see a homeless person with a cardboard sign. I see a person whom God loves, with a story I simply don't know. I also recognize that God's grace is often mysteriously ministered to *two* people at the same time.

Though there are times when God calls us to do something fairly radical to help a person in pain, most of the things God asks us to do are relatively small things. These involve being more aware, looking *at* people rather than through them. To realize that everyone is carrying a heavy load, and a word of kindness and encouragement can make all the difference to a brother or a stranger, a spouse or a child, or an aging parent. It's a cup of cold water or hot soup in his name, as Jesus whispers to us to take a little action here and there, now and again, on our daily journey. In the giving, whether from a place of fullness or emptiness, I am blessed, and you will be too.

## God's Way to Satisfaction

Though our culture barrages us with messages like "You deserve a break today," and instructs us to "Obey your thirst"—insisting that the way to life is in getting what we want—the message of Jesus suggests a very different way to satisfaction. In a kingdom economy, the first is last and the last first. The one who gives his life away finds it, and the one who doggedly grips his life loses it. It is the counterintuitive way of this upside-down kingdom, where Jesus says we will find the life that truly *is* life. These confounding words that he spoke, he also lived out to give us a glimpse of the good life—eternal life.

On the night before he would be crucified, Jesus gathered with his disciples to share a meal with them, teach them, and equip them for what was to come. It was then that he stooped to serve them by washing their feet. Knowing how the lesson might easily get lost, Jesus marked the moment with a clear instruction: "A new command I give you: Love one another. As I have loved you, so you must love one another. By this everyone will know that you are my disciples, if you love one another" (John 13:34–35).

This is a gracious command. Hidden in it is this surprising grace: As we serve, God meets us in mysterious ways.

## The Way of the Wise

Recent research has shown that participating in community service activities and helping others has healing effects in the lives of addicts and alcoholics. Long before these statistics were tabulated, the founders of Alcoholics Anonymous had already discovered the same thing.[2]

In the pages of *The Big Book of Alcoholics Anonymous* is told the tale of two friends, both alcoholics, struggling together to stay sober.[3] Aware that they needed to stay spiritually active, the two phoned the head nurse at a local hospital and inquired as to whether the facility might have an alcoholic in need of their help. They were in luck! She explained, "Yes, we've got a corker. He's just beaten up a couple of nurses. Goes off his head completely when he's drinking."

One of the men instructed the nurse: "Put him in a private room. We'll be down."

Two days later, the man welcomed the two strangers. When they explained that they were there to treat him for alcoholism, the man's face fell. Disheartened, he explained, "Oh, but that's no use. Nothing would fix me. I'm a goner. The last three times, I got drunk on the way home from here. I'm afraid to go out the door. I can't understand it."

His friends didn't scold him, didn't lecture him, and didn't shame him. Instead, they sat beside him and shared stories of their own experiences with alcohol. Story after story, the man listened. And little by little, he saw himself in their stories.

Still, he couldn't get over his shame. Believing he was hopeless and that they were wasting their time, he urged them to go. But they didn't go. They stayed and continued to share their experiences, this time not only their experiences with alcohol but of an awareness that came to them through a spiritual awakening that helped them to see their alcoholism in a different light.

At the mention of spiritual things, the man hardened, and his friends finally left. But not for long.

By the next day, the man had softened. "Maybe you're right," he said. "God ought to be able to do anything." Then he added, "He sure didn't do much for me when I was trying to fight this booze racket alone."[4] By the third day, he relinquished his life to the care and direction of his Creator. Living a life of sobriety, he became active in the church and helped other alcoholics find hope.

*The Big Book* explains, "So, you see, there were three alcoholics in that town, who now felt they had to give to others what they had found, or be sunk."[5]

What apt language! When they extended an arm to help another who was drowning in poison, they were kept afloat by a power greater than themselves. Thanks be to God!

*The Big Book* explains, "Though they knew they must help other alcoholics if they would remain sober, that motive became secondary. It was transcended by the happiness they found in giving themselves for others. They shared their homes, their slender resources, and gladly devoted spare hours to fellow-sufferers."[6] Through service to others, the men were transformed. Not only did they remain sober—"afloat" as it were—but they experienced deep happiness as their lives were poured out for others. That the description of their giving sounds much like the first-century church—sharing homes and resources with those in need—can be no coincidence.

New research is also demonstrating that those with eating disorders are buoyed by service to others. Noticing that these sufferers, who often see themselves in a negative light, have a heightened self-focus, professionals began to wonder whether the pursuit of self-esteem—increasing focus on the self—was as *valuable* to recovering from eating disorders as once thought. Shifting away from encouraging individuals to pursue self-esteem, many are now inviting those battling eating disorders to shift their focus outward by serving others. In fact, studies are already showing that those who are contributing to others are less likely to experience depression and anxiety.

Isn't this marvelous? God's good design is that we find peace and wholeness as we pattern our lives after Jesus by giving ourselves to one another.

## Seemingly Impossible Possibilities

The temptation, of course, for those of us struggling to carry our own load, is that we will simply be unable to bear the burden of another. In *One Thousand and One Thoughts From My Library*, Dwight L. Moody cites the wisdom of author George S. Merriam who conjectures,

> When your burden is heaviest, you can always lighten a little some other burden. At the times when you cannot see God, there is still open to you this sacred possibility to show God; for it is the love and kindness of human hearts through which the divine really comes home to men, whether they name it or not.[7]

He's confirming that in the darkest of times, we are still able to serve as conduits of God's love. Merriam continues on to exhort, "Let this thought, then, stay with you: there may be times when you cannot find help, but there is no time when you cannot give help."[8] It is in this giving that we come to experience, in an almost mystical way, the presence and support of a loving God.

> Then the King will say to those on His right, "Come, you who are blessed of My Father, inherit the kingdom prepared for you from the foundation of the world. For I was hungry, and you gave Me *something* to eat; I was thirsty, and you gave Me *something* to drink; I was a stranger, and you invited Me in; naked, and you clothed Me; I was sick, and you visited Me; I was in prison, and you came to Me."
>
> Then the righteous will answer Him, "Lord, when did we see You hungry, and feed You, or thirsty, and give You *something* to drink? And when did we see You a stranger, and invite You

in, or naked, and clothe You? When did we see You sick, or in prison, and come to You?"

The King will answer and say to them, "Truly I say to you, to the extent that you did it to one of these brothers of Mine, *even* the least *of them*, you did it to Me."

Jesus (Matthew 25:34–40 NASB)

# 12

# Peace in God's Creation

> The best remedy for those who are afraid, lonely, or unhappy is to go outside, somewhere where they can be quiet, alone with the heavens, nature, and God.[1]
>
> Anne Frank

Swarms of small children walked among cages and aquariums featuring hairy crawling spiders and creepy slithering snakes. Toddlers pressed sticky noses and fingers against the glass for a closer look at a tarantula or oversized cockroach. In the midst of the displays that are the stuff of some folks' nightmares, was a single tank filled with the most dazzling wet creatures. Perched on rocks, hiding under leaves, was a tank full of poison dart frogs.

Named for the animal's toxic secretion, which can be used to poison the tips of weapons, the small, slimy frogs are among the most wonderful splashes of whimsy and vibrant color in

God's creation. Native to Central and South America, they're wrapped in brightly painted and decorated skins. One species is a brilliant color of blue, its back splattered with black dot markings. Another is a brilliant red with bright blue legs—like a Marvel Comics superhero! One variety is black, covered in wavy yellow stripes with black polka dots on the stripes. Others, in brilliant shades of bright teal, electric lime green, and deep orange explode with creative design. As I made a note to never step on one in the wild, these dazzling creatures reflect the glory, splendor, and imagination of a God of beauty.

## Wonders Upon Wonders

Perhaps you're not inspired by amphibians. What is it that, by its very wonder, moves you to worship God? Is it the bold pattern of a zebra? Is it the soft belly of a curled-up sleeping kitten? Is it the zest of a lemon? Is it the glory of a rainbow? Is it the song of a chirping bird?

More specifically, where have you recognized God's presence in nature? When you've been caught in an unexpected downpour, being pummeled by sheets of relentless rain? Understandably, it may not be in the rain. If you've ever been caught in rough weather while camping, you may instead celebrate God's remarkable design in the shelter of a cave or a cliff. If your boat has capsized on a winding river, and you've paused to dry out supplies, the parting of clouds that allow healing sunlight to bathe you and your gear may be God's gift to you. When you've lost electricity during an ice storm, the simple glow of a candle or crackling of a warm fire reveals the mighty Creator.

The child of an acquaintance had to undergo the amputation of one foot, and later the other due to a disabling condition at birth. These surgeries would, doctors promised, allow the child greater mobility via prosthetics, which would enable him to walk and run for the first time in his life. In the process, learning about the internal blood supply systems that would maximize healing, my friend was moved to awe at the intricacy of the human body. In the midst of a storm she never would have chosen, she could recognize God's amazing handiwork in the human design.

When we open our eyes and our hearts to see God's wonder, we recognize his steadfast presence, even as the winds blow.

## Natural Reservations

I have one friend who is dubious, to put it mildly, about the possibility that God could be found in nature. To Don's ear, it rings as an excuse not to find God where he seems to be most clearly revealed. A man of strong faith, Don recognizes God's powerful presence in the Scriptures, in prayer, and in the body of Christ, but he struggles to recognize the particularity of this God in creation.

Don explained to me, "When my mom would take us to church each week, my dad would pack up his golf clubs and head across town to meet his buddies. When my brother and I protested his absence, he'd always say, 'I meet God on the golf course. I see God in nature.'" Even as a boy, my friend didn't buy it. "The only person my dad convinced," he explained, "was himself."

To recognize God's presence in the natural world is not to *dodge* God, to know *less* of God. Rather, to see God's majesty in a dew drop clinging to a bloodred tulip petal, to marvel at the whimsical coloring of the ladybug, or to be awestruck as a bright hot orb of sun dips behind the horizon is to know *more* of God. It's a way to explore more deeply the rich character of the Almighty. God's intricate handiwork in the natural world *illumines* what we know to be true of God through Scripture, in prayer, and via the body of Christ.

## Genesis Creation

As the Scriptures open with the marvelous account of God's great acts of creation, we're given an intimate gift of God's character through what he has made.

In creating light, God dispelled the thick gloom of darkness. In providing fruit and grain, God is revealed as a generous and faithful Provider. In filling the sea with an endless variety of swimming and slithering creatures, God's abundance and imagination were displayed. In giving birds flight, God's intricate engineering was given glorious form. And in the pinnacle masterpiece of God's creation, in the sculpting of man, God's own image became flesh. In the beauty and intricacy, genius and wonder of God's creation, the very character of God is revealed.

As we look around at what God has made, we're able to see *something of who He is*. The author of Psalm 19 points to the veracity of nature's God-revealing power:

> The heavens declare the glory of God;
> the skies proclaim the work of his hands.
> Day after day they pour forth speech;
> night after night they reveal knowledge.

They have no speech, they use no words;
no sound is heard from them.
Yet their voice goes out into all the earth,
their words to the ends of the world.
Psalm 19:1–4

That God's voice echoes through what God has made is a little bit different than golfing on Sunday mornings. Rather, the psalmist recognizes in creation the presence and power of the One who, in the beginning, created. To "find" God in nature is to recognize the God of the Christian Scriptures who longs to be known.

## Nature Testifying to God's Faithfulness

In my experience, it is in the midst of the storm when God's presence through nature often speaks the loudest. I'm fairly certain the old boat-builder Noah would testify to this in a heartbeat! After he'd been instructed to build the world's first RV, a huge floating ark, which would become a summer home for Noah's family and the motley zoo that was God's creation, the mighty storm began. "On that day," the Scripture says, "all the springs of the great deep burst forth, and the floodgates of the heavens were opened" (Genesis 7:11). Can you imagine? It wasn't just raining from the skies. It was raining from the *ground* as well! For forty days and forty nights Noah and his kin endured what must have felt like an interminable storm.

If Moses had ever been impressed with God's handiwork in sculpting the majestic mountains, his perspective would have been shifted as the waters lifted his home high above the altitude where the mountain caps had been. After forty days of storm, and even more days being held captive by the waters, Noah's ark landed on solid ground. Sending out a dove from the ark, Noah waited for its return. Don't you think Noah thanked God for the olive leaf when the dove returned with the plucked leaf in its beak, signaling the presence of dry land? What a glorious sign of hope and redemption.

There would, though, be one more sign to buoy Noah's spirits in the wake of the storm. On the day in which God created a covenant with Noah, the Lord promised never to destroy the earth again by flood. To mark his covenant, God spanned the heavens with a glorious rainbow, promising, "Whenever the rainbow appears in the clouds, I will see it and remember the everlasting covenant between God and all living creatures of every kind on the earth" (Genesis 9:16). In God's covenant with Noah, and with the generations who would follow, nature itself bore witness to God's steadfast, faithful love in a brilliant splash of color streaked across the sky.

## Entering Into Creation

Besides bearing signs of God's presence and provision, nature can also bring a visceral heart-calming peace to the physical body in the midst of chaos.

Many who suffer from seasonal affective disorder (SAD), who are negatively impacted by the dull, deadening gray of winter, find physical and emotional relief from suffering through nature. For these, being exposed to either the sun's healing rays or, in their absence, a man-made replication is to receive God's good gift! In this dynamic healing therapy, creation itself ministers to the body and minds of the suffering ones God loves.

In less dramatic ways, our bodies receive other types of comfort from God. For example, those who are chronically distracted by the urgency of cell phone messages, pressing texts, full email inboxes, and troubling tweets, who choose to *unplug*, find soothing relief beside a babbling brook. Calmed by the rippling rhythm of nature, the tyranny of the urgent ceases to reign.

Some of my friends whose bodies are bound by physical disability have found unusual freedom in pools and oceans and swimming holes. Though constrained by the constant conflict between uncooperative muscles and the desire to move against gravity through space, these friends taste God's gift of freedom and buoyancy and life in the water.

Even food becomes God's natural gift to those enduring stormy seas. Berries, replete with vitamin C, have proved helpful in combating stress. When German researchers asked 120 people to give a speech and do hard math problems—clear stressors!—those who'd received vitamin C had lower blood pressure and lower levels of the stress hormone.

The gift of peace in the storm, the gift of calm is, in so many quiet ways, woven into God's good gift of creation.

## The Gift of Palmer Lake

The beautiful spot on this earth where I've had glorious access to God's presence and peace through nature is the Palmer Lake Reservoir in Palmer Lake, Colorado. It's where I spent time with my grandson last summer, but more often, I go there for solitude. When I had an office near there, I'd hike up the trail to enjoy the quiet by the lake. I would experience God's palpable presence with me as I simply sat resting or in prayer.

Each season on the trail had its own comfort, and winter was my favorite. Because very few folks hiked there in the winter, I'd often have the entire landscape to myself. With the snow absorbing every sound, the air was still, calm, serene. During days and weeks when my hands were busy, my mind was full, and my heart was crowded, the gift of that spacious beauty blessed me beyond measure.

Has there been, for you, a spot in the natural world where you've known God's presence with you in a palpable way? Perhaps it was a reflective spot you remember from summer camp as a child. Or maybe during college you found a haven where you could steal away to study or rest. Or perhaps there is a vacation you're dreaming of right now—a beach, a lake, a forest—where you intend to meet God, to receive his comfort.

If you don't have a location in mind, begin to ask God where you might find respite and peace with him. While the shores of Grand Cayman may inspire, your place of solitude doesn't need to *cost* anything. You can find quiet on a local nature trail or state park. Perhaps you know of a river or a quarry tucked in the woods. Or perhaps there is simply a walking trail near your home where, away from the swirl of responsibilities, you can meet with God.

## Mighty Waters

In addition to Palmer Lake in the crisp coolness of winter, throughout my lifetime, I've often found God's peaceful presence in my encounters near water.

As a young boy, I loved going to the Trinity River in southeast Texas. Long before the Corps of Engineers tamed the river with its levies, I spent many imaginative hours along the river. I'd try to read the tracks the animals had left from the night before. Imagining the treasures I could discover, I hunted for fossils. I fished along the bank and skipped rocks across the surface of the water. Like a genuine cowboy, I shot my slingshot or pellet gun. The land alongside the river was, for me, a place where I could be whoever I wanted to be. It was a true gift.

At fifteen, the summer before my sophomore year in high school, I went canoeing in Canada with other boy scouts. After paddling our way up the river for the day, we stopped to make camp for the night near a cliff called Eagles' Nest. Around sunset, we scaled the height to take in the view. Long streaks of gold scraped the sky. Loons called to one another. The scene was so incredibly peaceful, it felt surreal. There I had a deep sense of God's mighty presence.

Another spot that brings reliable calm to my spirit is any beach on the ocean. The lapping of waves, foaming into silence, has always eased my anxieties. When I have the opportunity to be at the beach, I thank God for his nearness and the visceral awareness of his presence with me.

## Given Eyes to See

One day, when author John Acuff was reading in Scripture about Moses encountering the burning bush, he found himself startled by Exodus 3:3: "So Moses thought, 'I will go over and see this strange sight—why this bush does not burn up.'" Moses, curious, hedged a little closer to investigate the mystery that God had ordained. Inspired by Moses' curiosity, the way he was drawn to God by noticing a most unnatural occurrence in nature, Acuff began to pray, "God, give me strange sights in my own life. Please give me mysteries to explore."[2] Recognizing the mystery of God, he asked for his eyes to be opened to discover the wonder of God in what God has made. This type of prayer is one that opens our eyes to God in ways we might not notice otherwise.

This is exactly the kind of vision displayed by the author of Psalm 19, one that recognizes and delights in God's visible presence through what he has made. My friend who doubts that God can be seen or known through nature would have had an argument on his hands with this guy! In the mysterious riddle of creation, all that God has made *speaks* without words. Within the giant canopy of space, the glory of God is proclaimed.

## Opening Your Eyes

Where is that particular revelation in nature where God's presence and glory are most evident to *you*? If you're like me, it may be in the psychedelic design of an animal like the dart frog. Or, like my friend, it may be in the marvelous intricacy of the human design. It may be in a dancing tongue of fire or the distant sparkle of the galaxies.

It may be that in the darkness of your own storm it has been hard to focus your eyes on God's promises in Scripture. Your ears, having taken on water, make you strain to hear the once-familiar strains of God's quiet voice speaking to your heart. Drenched, even the warmth God has provided through brothers and sisters in the body of Christ feels very far away.

Beloved, know that God longs to meet you and comfort you with his presence. As you open the eyes of your heart to receive him, it may be through the wonders he has created. It could be that, in the midst of chaos, God will provide a natural anchor to give you *shalom* in the storm.

## Navigating With Nature

One of the risks of traveling by sea is that sudden storms can come up without warning. Dizzied and bounced about, as when chaos strikes in our own lives, ancient sailors were at risk of becoming disoriented and lost. Though most could recognize the familiar landmarks near home—the preciseness of a reef or the curve of the shore—leaving familiar waters was a risky venture.

If they were to remain on course, the only navigational anchors available to them were those in the sky. By day they could see the sun, by night the stars. When sailors could locate their position in relation to these reliable guides, they'd be able to head toward home. If the compasses they depended on for direction lost their magnetic charge, sailors had only to rely on a single point fixed directly over the North Pole. When they located the North Star, they'd be able to chart an effective course in relation to their location.

In the storm you're facing, it may be that rains have clouded your vision. Anchorless, you are adrift. Darkness has fallen and maps have failed. The glowing orb of God's presence that once seemed so radiant in your daytime journey has dipped behind the horizon. Now desperate, seeking, you're searching for some semblance of direction.

Beloved, lift your eyes to the heavens, to the reliable Guide who longs to bring you guidance and peace.

Your unfailing love, O LORD, is as vast as the heavens;
your faithfulness reaches beyond the clouds.
Your righteousness is like the mighty mountains,
your justice like the ocean depths.
You care for people and animals alike, O LORD.
How precious is your unfailing love, O God!
All humanity finds shelter
in the shadow of your wings.

Psalm 36:5–7 NLT

# 13

# Peace Through Recreation

> The word *recreation* is really a very beautiful word. It is defined in the dictionary as "the process of giving new life to something, of refreshing something, of restoring something." This something, of course, is the whole person.[1]
>
> Bruno Hans Geba

For almost 130 years, Coca-Cola has been producing new slogans to inspire thirsty drinkers everywhere to reach for the cool brown fizzy liquid. At the product's inception, in 1886, the product's tagline was simply "Drink Coca-Cola." It was nothing if not straightforward. In 1904, the company appealed to consumers' senses with advertisements claiming, "Delicious and Refreshing." The following year, makers upped their claim with "Coca-Cola Revives and Sustains." The year in which a worldwide depression infected America, 1929, Coke manufacturers appealed, "The Pause that Refreshes." In the midst of deep darkness, the promise of refreshment could be purchased in a 12-ounce bottle.

## Sustainable Solutions

When my bloodstream needs a little caffeine and sugar boost, Coca-Cola does the trick. I've also noticed that my body, mind, and spirit have deeper needs for refreshment that truly satisfies. Sometimes, when I've been writing for hours, my brain struggles to find the right words in a way it hadn't early on. Or there are times when I've been wrestling with a personal problem, mine or someone else's, that I simply can't solve. All the analyzing in the world won't cause the difficulty to budge an inch. Or perhaps I've been working in the yard all morning without food or drink. While a Coke might be a start, my body craves hydration *and* nourishment that will truly sustain.

The very first psalm in the Bible's combination prayer-book-hymnal describes the person who is refreshed and sustained, in the deepest way, by the Lord:

> That person is like a tree planted by streams of water,
> which yields its fruit in season
> and whose leaf does not wither—
> whatever they do prospers.
>
> Psalm 1:3

This type of bone-deep refreshment isn't a five-hour energy boost. Rather, the Lord offers nourishment that sustains over the long haul. God knows how we are made and that our temptation to be godlike is manifest in ways that tap our resources. We work long hours at the office. We give ourselves in caring for family members—young and old—to the neglect of our own bodies. We dutifully serve our church, sometimes crushed by the stress of too many commitments.

Beloved, this is not the Father's good will for your life. Rather, God longs for you to know the respite and rest and refreshment he offers.

## Pause to Refresh

A creative friend of mine had been struggling to perfect her website and was at her wit's end, ready to crush her laptop with a sledge hammer. She emailed a tech-savvy friend who asked her if she'd been refreshing her browser.

"What?" my friend asked, imagining spraying a light mist onto the screen of the machine that had become her arch nemesis.

"Just push Control and R at the same time," her helper typed back.

Dubious, my friend tried it. And like magic she was looking at a new Web page that reflected all the work she'd put into it throughout the day.

"Control R!" my friend bellowed to an empty house. The simple command had changed the most frustrating piece of her professional life.

"Control R" stands for "Refresh." It's what clears away the old information and replaces it with the new. What's true of machines, like my friend's laptop—that they are able to produce and display new information when the old is discarded—is true for the human machine as well!

When we pause to refresh—even when we feel we can't afford to take a break—we find ourselves equipped with new resources.

ntrol R” looks different for each one of us. For some it means engaging with nature, spending time hiking, fishing, or hunting. They might unfold a beach chair, dig it into the seaside sand, and soak in the warmth of God’s rays. Others might relax on a sofa with a book or watch a favorite television show or movie. Others might be recharged by heading out to the theater or a fine restaurant. And somewhat counterintuitively, many find new energy as they *expend* energy! The rhythmic pace of walking, biking, jogging—or even jumping on a neighbor’s trampoline—releases endorphins that lubricate brains and bodies to face obstacles with fresh energy.

## The Master Design

One of the creative ways parents discipline small children is to give them a time-out. If a little girl has pushed her brother, she might be asked to sit on the porch steps for five minutes while others continue to play. If a boy has spoken unkindly to a friend, he might need to sit on a kitchen stool to cool down. The wisdom of the time-out is that a child is given a chance to regain his composure for the purpose of returning to the work of being a kid—playing and running and building—as one who is refreshed and restored.

## Made to Be Re-Created

Though children give it their best shot, until they fall asleep at the dinner table or come unglued with a friend, God has designed us all as machines, to be moving at full-throttle throughout the day and night. In fact, God's good intention for us to be recharged is woven into creation itself. When God created the heavens and the earth, sun and moon, swimming fish and flying birds, God saw that it was good. And on the seventh day, having punched his time card, headed home, and slid out of his work clothes, God *rested*.

Later, when God would command the same Sabbath rest for human beings, it was for the express purpose of refreshment:

> Six days you shall do your work, but on the seventh day you shall rest; that your ox and your donkey may have rest, and the son of your servant woman, and the alien, may be refreshed.
>
> Exodus 23:12 ESV

It was a pervasive rest that was meant to recharge not only the strong, not only wealthy landowners who could afford to kick up their heels, but even their servants and animals were given space to recharge as well.

The cyclical rhythm of refreshment isn't just built into the macro plan—into the pause that God and creation take one day out of seven—it's also coded into the human design to be experienced every twenty-four-hour period. It's called sleep!

On more than one occasion I've fallen asleep with a heavy heart or racing mind, only to wake and find a new dimension of relief from my burdens.

When we agree to cooperate with God's rhythm for our lives, we enjoy the abundant refreshment God promises as we release our work and trust in his goodness. When we do, we're at times surprised by what is born. Rest and sleep are just one way to do this. There is also joyful activity that feeds our brains and souls with happy energy for the work we are called to do.

Time-outs aren't just for kids! We all need time-outs so our brains and bodies can reboot.

## The Aha! Moment

Do you ever wonder how inventors get their ideas? Have you ever been curious how scientists researching cures for deadly diseases come up with the break that cracks the problem wide open? Do you ever think about what sparks the imagination of a novelist or artist or songwriter? While it's certainly not a linear process, patterns can be recognized in the way human beings come up with new ideas and discoveries.

When faced with a conflict or searching for a solution, one of the stages of discovery is an interlude for scanning. For example, perhaps we've been crammed in an airline seat, puzzling over a Sudoku game at the back of an in-flight magazine. Or maybe we've been staring at a visual puzzle on the back of a cereal box. Or we're searching for the name of an acquaintance we've noticed in the grocery store before we have to actually stop and chat. The period in which we're searching for the name, searching for a solution, is the interlude for scanning.

As I'm sure you've experienced, whether searching the files of your memory banks or trying to make connections that lead to a new insight, this doesn't always happen in a timely fashion! What often happens, instead, when we aren't able to come up with a solution, is that we take a break.

Then later, sometimes at the most unlikely or inconvenient time, the solution will suddenly appear with force and insight. We may wake from a dream and suddenly know the answer to the cereal box puzzle. We might be enjoying the salty snacks and soda the flight attendant has brought us and then, returning to the puzzle, the answer seems entirely obvious. Perhaps we smile and wave across the produce section because we weren't able to come up with the name of our grocery store acquaintance. Then, several days later, the name simply pops into our minds.

The interlude for scanning, the rest and refreshment our brains need to function, is the human equivalent of "Control R"!

God has designed these amazing brains to function in ways we don't fully understand. What we do know is that when we give our bodies and brains the chance to relax and be refreshed—through rest or recreation—we are recharged to be in the world in fresh ways. Like the pair of AA rechargeable batteries pressed into a wall charger, we're strengthened to function again in the world when we pause to be refreshed.

That summer I spent with my grandson, swimming and eating brownies and watching *Toy Story 3*, was a precious season that recharged my batteries. The time I spent in the presence of this marvelous little boy—wondering at what caused him wonder, celebrating his first swimming strokes, laughing at what he found funny—was used by God to re-create me in ways I am not fully able to describe.

## Permission to Play

Sometimes, as Christians, we have trouble giving ourselves time to enjoy recreation. We balk at offering ourselves permission to take care of ourselves. Whether or not we identify as Protestant, many of us have internalized the Protestant, or Puritan, work ethic that points to hard work, and the prosperity that is supposed to flow from it, as signs of a person's salvation. And though we might not like to admit it in good company, too often we behave in just this way. We accept too many responsibilities at church. We volunteer too many hours in the community. We may even serve our families to the extent that it is no longer healthy for us or for them. Perhaps we'll even scoff at those we see engaging in what we deem to be frivolous activity: shopping or bowling, playing Frisbee or solitaire. "Don't they have better things to *do*?" we might demand in the quiet of our hearts.

When we guffaw at those who embrace recreation, we find ourselves in biblical company! Folks who were unable to recognize God's chosen one said of *Jesus*, "Here is a glutton and a drunkard, a friend of tax collectors and sinners" (Matthew 11:19). What detractors meant to be derogatory is, to my ear, a reflection of the manner in which Jesus lived. Throughout the Gospels we see Jesus at work: teaching, preaching, healing, forgiving. We're also privileged to have this other glimpse of Jesus at play. In the bitter accusation, and in other moments of Jesus' life, we see him *enjoying* people. He made himself the lunch guest at the home of Zacchaeus the tax collector. He enjoyed merriment, even refreshing the supply of wine at a wedding. He grilled fish on the beach for his friends.

Because we've been created as individuals, the way in which we are refreshed and recharged is unique to each one of us. While one person might find cooking a four-course dinner to be terribly stressful, for another to do so would be a gift that brings new life. The same is true of physical activity. The five-mile run that would completely drain and demoralize one who's already struggling would blow fresh wind into the sails of another. One person might find the sounds and smells and crowds at a major league baseball game to be overwhelming, while another would happily blend into the tapestry and thoroughly enjoy the pleasure of being a spectator. One person might enjoy the comforting clickety-clack of knitting needles, stitching a long woolly scarf, and another would find refreshment in wearing that scarf to ski a black diamond run in the mountains of Colorado!

What does recreation look like in your life? What is that activity—either the one that soothes and relaxes or the one that fires and fuels—that allows you to refresh and recharge?

Far from being un-Christian, engaging in recreation might be the very thing into which God invites us to refresh and refuel and recharge so that—with gratitude!—our works offered in love *can* reflect the salvation God has given us.

I will refresh the weary and satisfy the faint.

Jeremiah 31:25

# Afterword

An old joke is told about a religious man, stranded on a rooftop during a raging flood. When a rescuer rows by in a boat to save him, the man replies, "No, I have faith that God will save me." The waters rise and another helper paddles by, begging him to get in the boat. Again the man of faith insists that because of his faith God will work a miracle. When the water is neck-high, a helicopter hovers overhead, ladder dangling, and a voice from a megaphone urges the man to grab on. Continuing to place his faith in God's salvation, the man refuses.

When the man drowns, he shows up at the pearly gates, more than a little miffed, demanding of Saint Peter: "Why didn't God save me?!"

Chuckling, Saint Peter answers, "We sent you two boats and a helicopter! What more did you want?"

It's *funny,* because the man was so clueless.

It's *true,* because *this is how God is.*

When life's storms rage, God does not abandon us. Rather, in the midst of the chaos, God graciously extends his salvation to those who turn to him. Perhaps a tsunami you could never have seen coming has rocked your world. Or maybe, right now, the age-old rains that have seemed to pummel you for a *lifetime* are raging mercilessly. Beloved, whatever storm you are facing today, you can be certain that God sees. God knows. God cares. If you're that person of faith who's stranded on a rooftop as the waters rise, God *is* your rescuer in the storm.

My prayer for you, as you face the rising waters, is that your eyes will be opened anew to recognize the myriad ways in which God is actively providing you peace. Perhaps you will recognize God's attentive presence in the face and voice of a steadfast friend. Or maybe you will hear God's voice as it leaps off the page and into your heart through the words of a psalm. God may comfort you in ways you've not experienced before—through the plot of a movie or storyline of a book—and God might also use the timeworn lyrics of a favorite old hymn to grant you peace.

Today, you may be *aching* to see God's marvelous miracle in the midst of circumstances you cannot control. This was the longing of the man who stood on a rooftop as the waters rose! And it may be that God's miracle *will* be witnessed as God changes the outward circumstances you face. The miracle God *guarantees*, however, is not that he'll calm the storm. It's that he'll calm his child. God's promise is that the peace of Christ, a peace we cannot fathom, descends upon us when everything else is falling apart.

Take my word on this, because I've *experienced it*. This miracle of the inner variety, this inexplicable and supernatural calm in the storm, is the greatest miracle you'll ever experience.

## Prayer:

*God of all power, as I face the raging waters today, I place my trust in you. Send your Spirit to open my eyes so that I might recognize your sure and certain rescue. Let my ears hear the soothing sound of your voice, even as the floodwaters rise. I put my trust in you, in the strong name of Jesus. Amen.*

# Notes

## Chapter 1: Peace Through Perspective

1. Charles H. Spurgeon, *All of Grace* (Norcross, GA: Trinity Press, 2013), 47.

## Chapter 2: Peace Through Prayer

1. Catherine Marshall, *Meeting God at Every Turn* (New York: Random House, Bantam Books, 1985).
2. St. Patrick, *The Confession of St. Patrick, from the original Latin with an Introduction and Notes,* trans., Thomas Olden (UK: Eremitical Press, 2010), 100–101.

## Chapter 3: Peace in the Hospitable Art of Listening

1. Henri Nouwen, *Reaching Out: The Three Movements of the Spiritual Life* (New York: Doubleday, 1986), 66.
2. Ibid., 55.
3. Carl Rogers, *On Becoming a Person: A Therapist's View of Psychotherapy* (Wilmington, MA: Houghton Mifflin, Mariner Books, 1995), 32.
4. John Fox, *Finding What You Didn't Lose: Expressing Your Truth and Creativity Through Poem-Making* (Los Angeles: Penguin Group, Tarcher, 1995), 58.
5. Dietrich Bonhoeffer, *Life Together* (New York: HarperOne, 2009), 97.

6. Philip Yancey, *Prayer: Does It Make Any Difference?* (Grand Rapids, MI: Zondervan, 2006), 159.

**Chapter 4: Peace Through Friends and Strangers**

1. Henri J. M. Nouwen, *Out of Solitude: Three Meditations on the Christian Life* (Notre Dame, IN: Ave Maria Press, rev. ed., 2004), 38.

**Chapter 5: Peace From God's Word**

1. A. W. Tozer, *The Pursuit of God* (Camp Hill, PA: Christian Publications, 1982), 9.

**Chapter 6: Peace in and Through Music**

1. Henry David Thoreau, *The Service,* F. B. Sanborn, ed. (Boston: Charles E. Goodspeed, 1902), 12.

2. Gavin Bryars, from the liner notes of his album *Jesus' Blood Never Failed Me Yet* (Label: Phillips, 1993). Text from the liner notes can be found at this site: http://www.gavinbryars.com/Pages/jesus_blood_never_failed_m.html. You can listen to the composition here: http://www.youtube.com/watch?v=hZZPMPPD2cI.

3. Corrie ten Boom, *Tramp for the Lord* (New York: Jove Books, 1986), 26.

4. William Cowper (1731–1800), "Sometimes a Light Surprises."

**Chapter 7: Peace Through Deep Rest**

1. Wayne Muller, *Sabbath* (New York: Bantam Books, 2000), 1.

2. Lauren F. Winner, *Mudhouse Sabbath* (Brewster, MA: Paraclete Press, 2008), 7.

3. http://www.reformjudaism.org/blog-tags/challah

4. As quoted in *Mudhouse Sabbath*, 2.

5. John 10; Psalm 23

6. ReformJudaism.com, http://www.reformjudaism.org/blog/2012/10/23/shabbat-home-ritual

**Chapter 8: Peace Through the Body of Christ**

1. Lloyd Cory, *Quote/Unquote* (Colorado Springs: Victor Books, 1977), 197.

2. You can read more of the Kents' story in Carol's memoir, *When I Lay My Isaac Down* (Colorado Springs, NavPress, 2004).

3. This version has been attributed to Mother Teresa, but variations of it have appeared in the writings of a number of other people. For an investigation into these variants, especially the version by Kent Keith, see: http://quoteinvestigator.com/2012/05/18/do-good-anyway/

## Chapter 9: Peace From a Balanced Brain

1. Charles Spurgeon, *When a Preacher Is Downcast* (Shining Light Publishing, 1970). The text of the sermon can be read online at: http://www.gotothebible.com/HTML/downcast.html.

2. John Grogan, *Marley & Me: Life and Love with the World's Worst Dog* (William Morrow, 2008), 170–171.

3. Ibid.

## Chapter 10: Peace From Insightful Books and Movies

1. Ingmar Bergman, *The Magic Lantern,* trans., Joan Tate (New York: Penguin Books, 1989), 73.

2. Vera Nazarian, *The Perpetual Calendar of Inspiration: Old Wisdom for a New World* (Australia: Spirit Publishing, 2010).

3. Harper Lee, *To Kill a Mockingbird* (New York: HarperCollins, 1960), 465.

## Chapter 11: Peace Through Serving Others

1. Alan Paton, *Instrument of Thy Peace: The Prayer of St. Francis* (New York: Seabury Press, 1975), 7.

2. Case Western Reserve University School of Medicine reports. In a review article published in *Alcoholism Treatment Quarterly*, Maria E. Pagano, PhD.

3. http://anonpress.org/bb/Page_156.htm

4. http://anonpress.org/bb/Page_158.htm

5. Ibid.

6. Dr. Bob Smith and Bill Wilson, *The Big Book of Alcoholics Anonymous* (2001), 159.

7. Dwight L. Moody, *One Thousand and One Thoughts From My Library* (originally published by Revell, 1898; Edition reprint, BiblioBazaar, 2010).

8. Ibid.

## Chapter 12: Peace in God's Creation

1. Anne Frank, *The Diary of a Young Girl* (New York: Random House, Bantam Books, 1993), 158.

2. http://www.jonacuff.com/stuffchristianslike/2009/02/486-finding-god-in-nature/

## Chapter 13: Peace Through Recreation

1. Bruno Hans Geba, *Being at Leisure, Playing at Life: A Guide to Health and Joyful Living* (UK: Leisure Science Systems International, 1985).

**Ken Gire** (ThM, Dallas Theological Seminary) is the author of twenty-five books, including the bestselling INTIMATE MOMENTS WITH THE SAVIOR series and *Windows of the Soul*. He has won two ECPA Gold Medallion Awards, and two of his titles were selected as C. S. Lewis Honor Books. Ken teaches weekend seminars on writing throughout the country. He lives in Baltimore, Maryland.

Learn more at www.facebook.com/kengire.